A Da Capo Press Reprint Series

**FRANKLIN D. ROOSEVELT
AND THE ERA OF THE NEW DEAL**
GENERAL EDITOR : FRANK FREIDEL
Harvard University

TRENDS IN
RELIEF EXPENDITURES
1910-1935

Division of Research
Work Projects Administration

Research Monographs

Works Progress Administration
Division of Social Research
Research Monograph X

TRENDS IN
RELIEF EXPENDITURES
1910-1935

By Ann E. Geddes

DA CAPO PRESS • NEW YORK • 1971

A Da Capo Press Reprint Edition

This Da Capo Press edition of *Trends in Relief Expenditures, 1910-1935,* is an unabridged republication of the first edition published in Washington, D.C., in 1937. It is reprinted by permission from a copy of the original edition owned by the Harvard College Library.

Library of Congress Catalog Card Number 74-166327
ISBN 0-306-70342-4

Published by Da Capo Press, Inc.
A Subsidiary of Plenum Publishing Corporation
227 West 17th Street, New York, N.Y. 10011
All Rights Reserved

Manufactured in the United States of America

TRENDS IN
RELIEF EXPENDITURES
1910-1935

WORKS PROGRESS ADMINISTRATION
Harry L. Hopkins, *Administrator*
Corrington Gill, *Assistant Administrator*
DIVISION OF SOCIAL RESEARCH
Howard B. Myers, *Director*

TRENDS IN RELIEF EXPENDITURES

1910-1935

By

ANNE E. GEDDES

•

RESEARCH MONOGRAPH X

1937

UNITED STATES GOVERNMENT PRINTING OFFICE, WASHINGTON

Letter of Transmittal

WORKS PROGRESS ADMINISTRATION,
Washington, D. C., July 15, 1937.

SIR: I have the honor to submit herewith a report entitled *Trends in Relief Expenditures, 1910–1935.* The object of this report is to give perspective to recent relief developments by relating them to long-time trends.

In the study are collected, for the first time, scattered and fragmentary data on outdoor relief expenditures prior to the recent depression. Taken singly, these relief series for individual States, cities, and groups of cities are too limited in coverage to warrant any generalizations concerning long-time relief trends in the United States. Taken together, they offer convincing evidence of a strong underlying upward trend in expenditures for at least two decades before the precipitous rise beginning in 1930. They show also a progressive tendency toward increased specialization in the forms of aid and relatively greater dependence on public than on private resources long before the period of Federal participation in emergency unemployment relief measures.

This report was prepared by Anne E. Geddes under the direction of Howard B. Myers, Director of the Division of Social Research, Works Progress Administration. Enid Baird and Franklin Aaronson cooperated in the preparation of the report. The Division of Research, Statistics, and Records, in addition to making available the basic statistical data for the FERA, the CWA, and the Works Program, prepared various special tabulations of the data for use in Part II of the report.

Acknowledgment is made to Ralph G. Hurlin of the Russell Sage Foundation and to Paul Webbink of the Social Science Research Council, who have rendered invaluable advisory and critical assistance.

Respectfully submitted.

CORRINGTON GILL,
Assistant Administrator.

Hon. HARRY L. HOPKINS,
Works Progress Administrator.

Contents

FIGURES

Trends in Relief Expenditures
1910-1935

INTRODUCTION

DURING THE recent depression, which has been of greater intensity and longer duration than any previous depression in the history of the United States, the relief of unemployment and distress has been a major national problem. The tremendous increase in the extent of need and the assumption by the Federal Government of a substantial share of the responsibility for meeting the need have focused attention on the administration of relief during the depression years and have made the general public aware of the issues involved.

Although much has been written concerning the scope and nature of the contemporary relief problem, little is known of the extent of the burden in the United States in the decades preceding the depression of the 1930's. The purpose of this study is to give as much perspective as possible to recent developments by viewing them in relation to long-time trends. The report is restricted to aid extended to families and individuals outside of institutions and does not include foster-home care or welfare services. The relief burden has been measured, in so far as possible, in terms of the amount of aid distributed to relief cases rather than in terms of the cost of relief plus its administration.

The term *relief* is a generic one covering many types and forms of aid. Since this report has been compiled from secondary sources, it has not been feasible to standardize terminology. Different terms designating the same or similar forms of relief have been used in the original sources and have been retained in the present discussion. *Outdoor relief* is an inclusive term in general use, referring to all types of relief extended to families and individuals outside of institutions. *Wage assistance* is a term devised especially for this report to refer to assistance of a modified relief character, extended in the form of wages to persons employed on the work programs operated during 1933, 1934, and 1935 by the Civil Works Administration, the Civilian Conservation Corps, the Works Progress Administration, and other agencies participating in the Works Program. An effort has been made to explain other terms as they arise and to make clear the distinctions between them.

This report is divided into two parts. Part I deals with the trend of public and private expenditures for outdoor relief in the quarter of a century from 1910 through 1935, while Part II develops trends for public assistance during the last 3 years of that period and incorporates both outdoor relief and wage assistance. The year 1910 was selected as a starting date for Part I because it is the earliest year for which any substantial body of relief data is available. The relief series in Part II have been extended only through 1935, the last full calendar year for which data were available at the time the report was prepared.

The task of the study has been to assemble and analyze existing relief series which would shed light on relief trends during the depression, and particularly during the period of Federal participation in financing and administering relief programs. No original collection of data was undertaken. The analysis presented is original, except in a few instances where findings have been abstracted or adapted from published sources with the permission of the authors and publishers. Acknowledgments and source references have been given in the text for such secondary material.

The analysis in Part I is purposely much fuller than that in Part II, since the various Federal agencies administering relief and assistance programs in recent years have individually published much statistical data concerning their operations.

Statistical data concerning the operations of the Federal Emergency Relief Administration; the Civil Works Administration, including the Civil Works Service; and the Works Program, exclusive of the Civilian Conservation Corps, were supplied by the Division of Research, Statistics, and Records of the Works Progress Administration. Data for the Civilian Conservation Corps were obtained from the Office of the Emergency Conservation Work and the Bureau of Labor Statistics. Data for the Resettlement Administration were obtained directly from that agency. The major contribution of Part II is to bring these data together in a readily accessible form and to combine them into an integrated relief and wage assistance series which will give a more complete measure of the total burden of public assistance, exclusive of institutional relief, than has hitherto been supplied.

Emphasis has been placed throughout the report on the measurement of expenditures for relief and wage assistance during the period covered. No attempt has been made to evaluate the effectiveness of the various relief measures in meeting need, to describe the policies or operations of the several agencies administering public assistance, or to interpret expenditure trends in terms of underlying economic or social conditions.

SUMMARY

AVAILABLE DATA on long-time relief trends have been assembled and analyzed in Part I of this report to supply a factual background of relief experience in the United States prior to the recent depression and the participation of the Federal Government in emergency relief activities. Information concerning past relief trends is limited for the most part to scattered data on relief expenditures in selected areas since 1910. The relief series presented cover various types of relief in different areas; they are exclusive of institutional relief and, as far as possible, of expenditures for administrative purposes.

The expenditure data for different areas show marked similarity in trend. Considered in conjunction with trends in relief legislation since 1910, they present a consistent picture of gradually increasing relief burdens prior to the precipitous upward movement in 1930. The assembled pieces of evidence are believed to support a number of conclusions concerning the trend of relief expenditures in the United States in the 26 years from 1910 through 1935. Although these generalizations have considerable historical significance, their greatest value lies in their bearing upon future developments. The following basic tendencies may be noted.

1. The forms of public relief have tended to become more and more differentiated through the enactment of special legislation.

2. There has been a progressive tendency to widen the base of governmental responsibility for relief beyond the local units, first through State and then through Federal participation.

3. At least since 1910 there has been a strong underlying upward trend in relief expenditures. The very great increase in expenditures in the depression years represents a sharp acceleration of a tendency manifest throughout the preceding two decades.

4. The increase in both public and private relief expenditures has been far greater than the growth in population.

5. The rate of increase of public relief expenditures, at least in large urban areas, has greatly exceeded that of all governmental expenditures combined.

6. While expenditures for general public relief have increased steadily, the most rapid expansion in public relief prior to the depression occurred in aid to dependent children.

7. There is little evidence that the introduction of aid to special classes, such as the aged, the blind, and dependent children, has resulted in the past in reduction of the general relief burden. Although there has been some shifting of cases from general relief rolls to the rolls of agencies providing statutory relief, to a considerable extent the special types of assistance have tapped new reservoirs of need. The influx of new cases to the general relief rolls, combined with rising standards of care, has largely offset such absorption as has occurred.

8. Following the 1921–1922 depression, relief expenditures did not return to the predepression level. There was a temporary recession from the depression peak but relief expenditures continued to mount in subsequent years.

9. There have been wide regional and local variations in the relative proportions of public and private relief, but public agencies bore an important share of the burden long before the onset of the recent depression. Since the assumption of a share of the responsibility for relief by the Federal Government in 1932 the proportion of the burden borne by private agencies has been very slight.

10. Work relief and work projects in the recent depression have assumed a new and increasing importance as a means of assisting the destitute unemployed.

11. The expansion in expenditures for outdoor relief has, since 1932, been relatively greater in rural and town areas than in urban areas.

PÀRT II

The evidence presented in Part I on outdoor relief expenditures in selected areas is supplemented in Part II by a more comprehensive record of public assistance expenditures in the United States as a whole in the years 1933, 1934, and 1935. During this period the Federal Government was participating in a variety of programs for the relief of unemployment and distress.

The series which are presented in Part I include public expenditures for general (emergency) relief and for categorical relief—i. e., for aid to the aged, aid to the blind, and aid to dependent children—but expenditures for wage assistance are not included.

In order to give a more complete measure of the total public assistance burden in this period an integrated relief series has been constructed which includes the three major classes of outdoor public aid: emergency relief, categorical relief, and wage assistance.

In 1933, 1934, and 1935 wage assistance constituted a very important part of the total public assistance structure. Expenditures for all forms of relief and wage assistance in this period totaled approximately $5,375,000,000. Of this amount more than 65 percent was for emergency relief, 30 percent was for wage assistance, and less than 5 percent was for categorical relief.

During the 3-year period there were frequent changes in Federal programs inaugurated for the relief of unemployment and distress, involving important shifts in emphasis from emergency relief to wage assistance and vice versa. There was also a very close interplay between the case loads of the emergency relief and the wage assistance programs. Hence, changes in one form of aid can be interpreted only in the light of changes in the other.

The following data are indicative of the effect on the public assistance structure of changes in program development. In January 1933 emergency relief constituted 91 percent of the total expenditures for outdoor public assistance, and wage assistance had not yet been developed as a means of meeting the needs of the unemployed. In January 1934 emergency relief had shrunk to 17 percent of the total while wage assistance constituted 81 percent. Emergency relief again accounted for the major share of expenditures in January 1935, with wage assistance only 10 percent of the total.

Throughout the 3-year period expenditures for categorical relief were fairly stable and constituted a very small proportion of the total burden.

The expenditure series in Part I and in Part II display wide differences in trend over the 36 months from January 1933 through December 1935. The peak of expenditures for emergency and categorical relief occurred in January 1935, while the peak of expenditures for these two forms of relief and wage assistance combined was reached a year earlier, in January 1934. In this month the Civil Works program was at its height and the emergency relief program was at its lowest ebb.

Any expenditure series necessarily supplies an imperfect measure of need. During the Federal period variations in the standards of care of the different emergency programs were very marked. Fluctuations in total expenditures, therefore, cannot be linked to fluctuations in the extent of need.

An integrated case series registering the total number of families and individuals receiving emergency relief, categorical relief, and wage assistance would serve as a far more sensitive and reliable index of the extent of need than an expenditure series. Unfortunately, reported data cannot be added directly to obtain an unduplicated case series for the entire 3-year period, although two estimated series representing households and individuals aided have recently been constructed.

The integrated expenditure series which has been developed for the United States is based on an aggregate of data for the 48 States, which had widely varied public assistance structures. The differences in State relief patterns suggest the need for developing integrated series for the separate States to supplement the national series which is presented here.

Part I

Outdoor Relief, 1910-1935

Part I

OUTDOOR RELIEF, 1910-1935

EMERGENCY RELIEF operations since midsummer of 1932, when the Federal Government first made funds available for relief, can be viewed in proper perspective only against a background of previous relief experience in the United States. Unfortunately, there are no Nation-wide statistics of the incidence, cost, and trend of relief operations before the period of Federal participation in relief.

AVAILABLE DATA ON LONG-TIME RELIEF TRENDS

Information available on long-time relief trends is limited principally to scattered data on relief expenditures covering different areas and different types of relief and extending over varying periods of time. Continuous data on case loads are entirely too fragmentary in coverage to establish past relief trends in terms of the number of cases receiving assistance. Individual public and private agencies have maintained records of case loads over long periods of time, and some significant case series have been developed, but combined case-load figures covering all agencies in given areas are conspicuously lacking.[1]

Although the early statistics on relief expenditures that have been assembled in this report are both crude and fragmentary and relate for the most part to large urban areas, when pieced together against a background of legislative trends, they tell a consistent story of relief costs in the past and help to illuminate the current relief situation. In brief, the story is one of continued expansion in relief expenditures for at least two decades before the beginning of Federal emergency relief activities for the unemployed. More liberal relief practices and new legislative provisions for public relief have contributed to the upward trend, but there is also evidence that the level of need has risen progressively higher with the passage of time. Relief expenditures have registered new peaks in business depressions and have not receded to their old levels with business recovery. Instead, after each depression they have again moved upward from a new and higher base.

---

[1] The most significant case series is that of the Department of Statistics of the Russell Sage Foundation covering the operations of selected family case-work agencies. This series was initiated in 1926.

The unprecedented scope of the recent depression and the participation of the Federal Government in unemployment relief have greatly accelerated the expansion in relief expenditures during recent years, but the effect upon relief trends has been primarily one of rate of change rather than of direction. The changes in types of relief and in distribution of the relief burden that have accompanied this rapid rise in relief expenditures have been more extensive in scope, but are not radically different in character from changes that have taken place over longer periods of time in the past.

Legislative Trends Affecting Relief Expenditures

Since relief trends are much affected by prevailing statutory provisions for public relief, it seems desirable to examine legislative trends in the States since 1910 to see how they have contributed to changes in the volume of relief and to throw some light on the origin and significance of the different types and forms of relief included in the composite relief series presented in later sections of the report.

Prior to the twentieth century, public outdoor relief in the United States was extended almost exclusively under the provisions of local poor laws, modeled for the most part after the English poor laws of Queen Elizabeth's time.[2] Many of these laws date from early Colonial days and have undergone only minor change during the intervening years. In some States the laws have been modernized and embody more progressive concepts of relief administration.

Traditionally a local responsibility, poor relief usually has been financed from local property taxes and dispensed by local overseers of the poor with little or no State supervision or control. Applicants for relief were frequently required to take a pauper's oath and to waive various political and civil rights as a prerequisite to receiving aid. The social stigma attached to poor relief has led gradually to the introduction of new statutory forms of relief for special classes who are in need obviously through no fault of their own or are deemed to have a special claim on society for consideration and care. Relief extended under these statutes to persons not in institutions has commonly been termed "categorical relief" or "aid to special classes,"[3]

---

[2] See Lowe, Robert C. and Associates, *Digest of Poor Relief Laws of the Several States and Territories as of May 1, 1936*, Division of Social Research, Works Progress Administration, 1936.

[3] Usage differs widely as to the designation of the statutory forms of assistance. Thus, relief for the needy aged is variously known as "aid to the aged," or "old-age assistance"; relief for dependent children in their homes as "aid to dependent children," "child welfare allowances," "aid to widowed mothers," or "mothers' aid"; and blind relief as "aid to the blind" or "blind assistance." Usage also differs regarding the inclusion of veteran relief as a form of categorical relief. In this report, the term "categorical" is confined to three special classes of statutory relief: aid to the aged, aid to the blind, and aid to dependent children. It is, therefore, synonymous with the term "special allowances" as used in the Urban Relief Series.

to distinguish it from general outdoor relief given to paupers in accordance with the local poor laws.[4]

Needy soldiers and sailors were among the first to benefit from special legislation. By 1910 all but six States had made statutory provision for relief of Civil War veterans. Many States had enacted similar laws providing relief to veterans of the Mexican, Indian, and Spanish-American Wars and the Boxer Rebellion. Since 1918 relief for World War veterans has been provided by statute in 30 States.[5]

Legislation for aid to the aged, aid to the blind, and aid to dependent children dates largely after 1910. The expansion of relief activities in the United States through the enactment of State laws providing assistance for these three special classes [6] is shown in appendix table 1, which gives the year of original enactment of enabling legislation for each of these forms of relief. Table 1 indicates by 5-year periods the spread of legislation for public assistance in their homes to the aged, to the blind, and to dependent children.

Table 1.—Number of States [1] Enacting First Legislation for Aid to the Aged, Aid to the Blind, and Aid to Dependent Children, in Specified Periods

Year of original enactment	Type of assistance		
	Aid to the aged	Aid to the blind	Aid to dependent children
All years	39	33	46
Before 1910	—	3	—
1910 through 1914	—	2	20
1915 through 1919	—	5	19
1920 through 1924	2	5	3
1925 through 1929	8	5	3
1930 through 1934	19	5	1
1935	10	8	—

[1] Includes the District of Columbia.

Illinois, Ohio, and Wisconsin enacted laws providing aid to the needy blind prior to 1910 but the further spread of such legislation was distributed over a wide span of years. A total of 33 States provided such aid by the close of 1935.

Aid for dependent children appeared somewhat later than blind relief, the first law being passed in Illinois in 1911, but this form of assistance spread more rapidly. Twenty States enacted laws of this type during the 5 years from 1910 through 1914, and nineteen States from 1915 through 1919. Only 7 of the 46 States [7] providing such aid in December 1935 introduced this form of legislation after 1919.

[4] It should be noted that in many localities individuals who might be eligible for some form of categorical relief, if there were legal provisions for it, still receive relief under the regular poor laws.

[5] Data on veteran relief legislation compiled by Robert C. Lowe, Division of Social Research, Works Progress Administration.

[6] For sources of data, see footnotes, appendix table 1.

[7] Including the District of Columbia.

The first laws authorizing aid to the aged were enacted in Montana and Nevada in 1923, but the period of greatest development in this type of legislation has been since 1930. Eight States enacted old-age legislation in the 5 years from 1925 through 1929, and nineteen States from 1930 through 1934. Under the stimulus of the Social Security Act 10 additional States passed laws during 1935, bringing the total number of States which had enacted old-age relief laws to 39.

The above tabulation gives an accurate picture of the spread of enabling legislation for categorical relief since 1910, but it cannot show important changes that have occurred in the application and coverage of the laws. In many instances, the date of enactment of a law does not coincide with the first year of operation. Furthermore, many of the State laws are, or were, optional in character and have been inoperative in many of the county units for part or all of the period since their enactment. Revisions in the laws, and qualitative changes in their administration and application, including eligibility requirements and the amount of assistance rendered, could be ascertained only by a survey of individual counties in the States with enabling legislation. The requirements of the Social Security Act that all counties must participate in extending relief to a particular category before the State can benefit from Federal grants-in-aid for that type of relief have induced many States to make their laws mandatory upon the county units and will contribute to the continued growth of expenditures for these forms of relief.

Simultaneously with the differentiation in the types of relief has occurred a gradual widening in the base of financial and administrative responsibility for relief activities.[8] This shift to larger governmental units has come about partly through a desire for more efficient administration and partly through the necessity of making available for relief purposes a greater variety of revenue resources than could be tapped by the local governments. Poor relief has, with few exceptions, remained a function of the local units. Veteran relief, on the other hand, was initiated and has been supported predominantly by the States. The newer forms of public assistance, including aid to the aged, to the blind, and to dependent children, have commonly been administered by county governments, with the State assuming partial or complete fiscal responsibility as well as a degree of supervisory control.

The extension, first to the States and then to the Federal Government, of part of the financial and administrative responsibility for unemployment relief was a logical step in this evolutionary process. Special legislation financing emergency unemployment relief was enacted in 14 States during 1931, or before the period of Federal

---

[8] See Lowe, Robert C. and Holcombe, John L., *Legislative Trends in State and Local Responsibility for Public Assistance*, Division of Social Research, Works Progress Administration, 1936.

participation. Four States made initial appropriations for unemployment relief in 1932. By the end of 1935, all but five States, Georgia, North Carolina, South Carolina, Vermont, and Virginia, had accepted some responsibility for providing State funds for unemployment relief.[9]

The practical effect of State and Federal participation in emergency relief activities was to bring almost to a halt in most localities the extension of outdoor poor relief by municipal and township units. The poor laws remained in effect but were virtually inoperative. With the withdrawal of the Federal Government from the support of direct relief at the end of 1935, extension of relief in many of the States reverted to the traditional poor laws, but a few States have merged unemployment relief activities with poor relief under permanent State Welfare Departments. It appears highly probable that other States will follow this example.

Sources of Statistical Data

For a long-time view of the public relief burden the most inclusive relief data are those on governmental-cost payments collected annually by the United States Bureau of the Census and published in *Financial Statistics of Cities*.[10] Additional data on relief expenditures over extended periods of years for public agencies and for public and private agencies combined are available for individual States, notably New York and Indiana, for individual cities, and for groups of cities.[11]

A special inquiry of the United States Bureau of the Census covering relief expenditures in 308 cities during the first quarters of 1929 and of 1931 has supplied 2 bench marks against which to measure the rise in relief expenditures during the recent depression.[12] The most comprehensive data on relief costs for the early depression years are supplied by the Urban Relief Series of the U. S. Children's Bureau.[13] This series is based on monthly data from 120 large urban areas and extends back to January 1929. A relief series for rural and town areas

---

[9] See appendix table 1 for dates of first legislation financing unemployment relief in individual States. For a complete record of such laws, see Lowe, Robert C., *Digest of State Legislation for the Financing of Emergency Relief, January 1, 1931–June 30, 1935*, Municipal Finance Section, Federal Emergency Relief Administration, and Lowe, Robert C. and Staff, *Supplement for Period July 1, 1935–February 29, 1936*, Division of Social Research, Works Progress Administration.

[10] U. S. Department of Commerce, Bureau of the Census, annual reports, *Financial Statistics of Cities Having a Population of Over 100,000, 1911–1931*.

[11] Sources for these data are given in footnote references at the beginning of the sections in which they are discussed.

[12] U. S. Department of Commerce, Bureau of the Census, special report, *Relief Expenditures by Governmental and Private Organizations, 1929 and 1931*, 1932.

[13] Winslow, Emma A., *Trends in Different Types of Public and Private Relief in Urban Areas, 1929–35*, Publication No. 237, U. S. Department of Labor, Children's Bureau, 1937. The Urban Relief Series was transferred to the Social Security Board as of July 1936.

was developed during 1936 by the Division of Social Research of the Works Progress Administration to complement the existing Urban Relief Series. Monthly data from these two series have recently been utilized by the Division of Social Research to establish the combined urban-rural trend of total relief expenditures in the United States since January 1932.[14]

The statistical data from these several sources are presented in succeeding sections of Part I to indicate the basis of generalizations that have been made concerning relief trends from 1910 through 1935. Long-time trends are treated first, followed by a more detailed analysis of changes since 1929.

TRENDS IN RELIEF EXPENDITURES IN SELECTED AREAS, 1910–1935

Governmental-Cost Payments for Outdoor Relief in 16 Cities, 1911–1931

An early relief series disclosing the upward trend of relief costs in 16 large cities from 1911 through 1931, the two decades preceding the period of Federal participation, has been developed for this study from data on governmental-cost payments for relief, collected by the Bureau of the Census and published in *Financial Statistics of Cities*. Governmental-cost payments include not only payments made to relief clients, but also the costs incident to the operation and maintenance of relief services.[15] Payments for "outdoor care of poor," "aid to soldiers and sailors," and "aid to mothers," separately recorded by the Bureau of the Census, have been combined into a single series for outdoor relief. Aid to the aged and aid to the blind are not separately tabu-

---

[14] See Division of Social Research, Works Progress Administration, *Current Statistics of Relief in Rural and Town Areas*, Vol. I, Nos. 1–10, 1936. Data for the combined Rural-Urban Series supplied in unpublished form by T. J. Woofter, Jr., Coordinator of Rural Research, Division of Social Research, Works Progress Administration. For methodology of combined series, see Woofter, T. J., Jr.; Aaronson, Franklin; and Mangus, A. R.: *Relief in Urban and Rural-Town Areas, 1932–1936*, Research Bulletin, Series III, No. 3 (in preparation), Division of Social Research, Works Progress Administration, 1937.

[15] The figures for governmental-cost payments include a share of county payments for relief as well as city payments. In 8 of the 16 cities for which data are given—namely, New York, Philadelphia, St. Louis, Baltimore, Boston, San Francisco, Washington, and New Orleans—county and city government units have been merged so that the figures collected automatically include both city and county payments. To insure comparability for the eight remaining cities, the Bureau of the Census has allotted to each city its share of county expenditures for the specified functions, prorating the county payments to the city in the ratio of assessed valuations of the city to assessed valuations of the entire county. A share of the county-cost payments has been allocated by the Bureau of the Census only to ciites in Groups I and II in which the city and county governments are not merged. The eight cities included here are the only ones with separate city and county governments which have been continuously in Group I or II since 1911. Thus, they are the only large cities for which comparable data are available for the full period.

lated by the Bureau of the Census, but are included with general poor relief in the figures for "outdoor care of poor." [16]

The 16 cities included in the series are widely distributed geographically and had a combined population according to the 1930 Census of 21,500,000, representing 17.5 percent of the total population and 31 percent of the urban population in the United States. Considerable significance can, therefore, be attached to the trend of relief costs for the group. The cities, listed in the order of size, are:

New York	Cleveland	Pittsburgh	Washington, D. C.
Chicago	St. Louis	San Francisco	New Orleans
Philadelphia	Baltimore	Milwaukee	Cincinnati
Detroit	Boston	Buffalo	Newark

Total governmental-cost payments for outdoor relief for the years from 1911 through 1931 supply evidence of a continuing rise in the public relief burden in these cities over the entire period, with the upward movement greatly accelerated after 1929.[17] Aggregate payments in the 16 cities amounted in 1911 to $1,559,000, in 1929 to $18,989,000, and in 1931 to $64,142,000; payments per inhabitant in these 3 years were $0.10, $0.90, and $2.94, respectively. Data for individual cities, given in table 2, show that every city except Washington, D. C., experienced an extensive rise in per capita relief costs over the 21-year period. The increase in Washington was comparatively slight. Governmental-cost payments for relief per inhabitant varied sharply in the different cities.

A breakdown of payments by class of relief indicates that expansion in "aid to mothers"[18] shares with "outdoor care of poor" the major responsibility for the accelerated growth of relief costs over the period. This rise in expenditures for aid to mothers, attributable to new legislative provisions, was particularly important prior to 1929. It is significant that despite the increase in amounts expended for this special category, there was no accompanying decline in expenditures for "outdoor care of poor," either in total amount or per inhabitant. Total governmental-cost payments for outdoor relief and payments per inhabitant for "aid to mothers," "aid to soldiers and sailors,"

---

[16] In *Financial Statistics of Cities*, "Outdoor Care of Poor" is a subdivision of Group VI, "Charities, Hospitals, and Corrections"; "Aid to Soldiers and Sailors" and "Aid to Mothers" are subdivisions of Group IX, "Miscellaneous Cost Payments." Aid to soldiers and sailors includes only relief and burial for needy veterans and does not include pensions or bonus payments; aid to mothers covers assistance in the home for the care of dependent children. It does not include such care in institutions.

[17] Data are for fiscal years ending during the calendar year. The annual collection of *Financial Statistics of Cities* was suspended by the Bureau of the Census for 2 years, 1914 and 1920; the collection was incomplete in 1921. For other years for which data are missing, the classifications were not uniform.

[18] Comparable to "aid to dependent children." See footnote 3, p. 2.

Table 2.—Governmental-Cost Payments for Outdoor Relief in 16 Cities, 1911–31 [1]

[Includes operation and maintenance costs]

City	1911	1912	1917	1918	1919	1923	1924	1925	1926	1927	1928	1929	1930	1931
Amount in thousands														
Total, 16 cities	$1,559	$1,700	$3,488	$3,980	$6,183	$11,640	$12,818	$14,709	$14,814	$17,059	$20,014	$18,989	$28,004	$64,142
New York	188	158	515	640	2,464	5,312	5,702	6,388	5,807	6,602	7,945	7,448	9,274	22,140
Chicago	327	407	592	734	824	1,132	1,253	1,389	1,443	1,688	1,985	1,546	2,120	3,379
Philadelphia	78	71	93	156	116	358	420	465	427	492	559	582	733	3,458
Detroit	112	118	339	400	447	969	1,051	1,514	1,674	2,485	2,944	2,393	5,935	14,851
Cleveland	143	122	177	175	187	288	242	277	313	295	368	446	480	1,899
St. Louis	1	1	68	94	109	190	191	221	241	243	258	282	152	251
Baltimore	10	17	17	18	16	122	114	116	124	170	165	171	219	493
Boston	332	363	879	913	1,004	1,600	2,004	2,223	2,176	2,244	2,601	2,889	4,235	7,187
Pittsburgh	53	38	47	52	74	135	159	165	162	199	410	375	411	935
San Francisco	12	17	145	164	168	278	255	250	618	281	306	314	415	645
Milwaukee	70	72	152	82	154	296	355	406	452	509	605	620	1,295	2,880
Buffalo	71	81	141	195	241	446	512	694	737	871	1,088	1,076	1,466	2,908
Washington, D. C.	30	27	28	24	23	19	26	21	25	29	28	29	48	49
New Orleans	6	6	11	16	15	12	13	17	17	276	51	29	22	67
Cincinnati	72	148	199	204	216	299	301	322	354	387	391	423	541	1,280
Newark	54	54	86	112	125	184	220	241	244	288	310	366	658	1,870
Amount per inhabitant [2]														
Total, 16 cities	$0.10	$0.11	$0.21	$0.23	$0.35	$0.62	$0.67	$0.75	$0.75	$0.85	$0.96	$0.90	$1.30	$2.94
New York	.04	.03	.09	.11	.45	.90	.98	1.09	.98	1.11	1.18	1.09	1.33	3.12
Chicago	.15	.18	.24	.29	.31	.39	.43	.46	.47	.54	.61	.46	.62	.98
Philadelphia	.05	.04	.05	.09	.07	.19	.22	.23	.21	.24	.29	.30	.38	1.76
Detroit	.23	.23	.56	.64	.47	.97	.90	1.24	1.32	1.89	2.08	1.61	3.82	9.17
Cleveland	.25	.20	.26	.25	.25	.32	.27	.30	.33	.30	.42	.50	.53	2.08

St. Louis	*	*	.09	.12	.14	.24	.24	.27	.29	.29	.32	.35	.19	.30
Baltimore	.02	.03	.03	.03	.02	.16	.15	.15	.15	.21	.21	.21	.27	.61
Boston	.48	.51	1.16	1.19	1.36	2.08	2.58	2.84	2.76	2.83	3.35	3.71	5.42	9.54
Pittsburgh	.10	.07	.08	.09	.13	.22	.25	.26	.25	.30	.62	.56	.61	.72
San Francisco	.03	.04	.31	.35	.34	.52	.47	.45	1.10	.49	.51	.51	.66	1.00
Milwaukee	.18	.18	.35	.18	.35	.61	.72	.80	.87	.96	1.11	1.09	2.23	4.86
Buffalo	.16	.18	.30	.41	.48	.84	.97	1.29	1.36	1.59	1.95	1.90	2.56	5.03
Washington, D. C	.09	.08	.08	.06	.05	.04	.05	.04	.05	.06	.06	.06	.05	.10
New Orleans	.02	.02	.03	.04	.04	.03	.03	.04	.04	.11	.06	.06	.05	.14
Cincinnati	.19	.38	.49	.49	.54	.74	.74	.79	.86	.94	.89	.94	1.20	2.80
Newark	.15	.15	.21	.27	.31	.42	.49	.53	.53	.62	.71	.83	1.49	4.19

*Less than $0.005.

¹ Data for fiscal years ending in calendar year. Data not available, or not available on a comparable basis, for the years omitted from this table.

² Based on annual population estimates of the Bureau of the Census.

Source: U. S. Department of Commerce, Bureau of the Census, annual reports, *Financial Statistics o¹ Cities Having a Population o²'Over 100,000, 1911–1931.*

and "outdoor care of poor"[19] in the 16 cities combined are shown in table 3.

Aggregate governmental-cost payments for all types of outdoor relief combined are compared in the accompanying diagram with payments for the maintenance and operation of all general governmental departments, and with growth in population. Although it is possible to establish trends over the period, there are certain definite breaks in the curves in years for which data are not available.[20] It is particularly

Table 3.—Aggregate Governmental-Cost Payments for Outdoor Relief in 16 Cities, by Class of Relief, 1911–1931[1]

[Includes operation and maintenance costs]

Year	Total	Outdoor care of poor	Aid to mothers	Aid to soldiers and sailors
Amount in thousands				
1911	$1,559	$1,042	$14	$503
1912	1,700	1,177	53	470
1917	3,488	1,801	1,054	633
1918	3,980	1,991	1,258	731
1919	6,183	2,139	3,317	727
1923	11,640	3,205	7,450	985
1924	12,818	3,699	7,986	1,133
1925	14,709	4,671	8,825	1,213
1926	14,814	5,415	8,261	1,138
1927	17,059	6,534	9,288	1,237
1928	20,014	7,364	11,201	1,449
1929	18,989	6,733	10,543	1,713
1930	28,004	13,553	11,430	3,021
1931	64,142	42,998	15,051	6,093
Amount per inhabitant [2]				
1911	$0.10	$0.07	*	$0.03
1912	.11	.08	*	.03
1917	.21	.11	$0.06	.04
1918	.23	.12	.07	.04
1919	.35	.12	.19	.04
1923	.62	.17	.40	.05
1924	.67	.19	.42	.06
1925	.75	.24	.45	.06
1926	.75	.27	.42	.06
1927	.85	.33	.46	.06
1928	.96	.35	.54	.07
1929	.90	.32	.50	.08
1930	1.30	.63	.53	.14
1931	2.94	1.97	.69	.28

* Less than $0.005.

[1] Data for fiscal years ending in calendar year. Data not available, or not available on a comparable basis, for the years omitted from this table.

[2] Based on annual population estimates of the Bureau of the Census.

Source: U. S. Department of Commerce, Bureau of the Census, annual reports, *Financial Statistics of Cities Having a Population of Over 100,000, 1911–1931.*

[19] Although "outdoor care of poor" includes some aid to the aged and to the blind, cost payments for these two special classes are believed to be relatively small until 1930. Of the 16 cities, only 3, Baltimore, San Francisco, and Milwaukee, gave aid to the aged prior to 1930. Aid to the blind is not an important category.

[20] The curves in this diagram are plotted on a semilogarithmic or ratio scale, and are therefore comparable for rate of change, although not for volume. The slope of the curves indicates the rate of change: the steeper the slope the greater the rate of change.

unfortunate that gaps in the relief curve occur in the depression years of 1914–1915 and of 1921–1922. However, data for public relief expenditures for these same and additional cities, compiled by Ralph G. Hurlin and shown later in this report, probably reflect what happened in the 1921–1922 depression period.[21]

It is apparent from figure 1 and from table 4 that relief payments mounted during the 21-year period at a much more rapid rate than

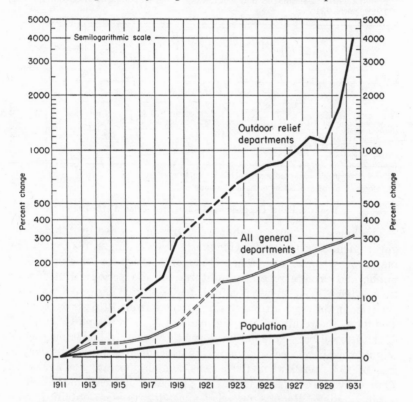

FIG. I – TRENDS OF POPULATION AND OF GOVERNMENTAL-COST PAYMENTS FOR OPERATION AND MAINTENANCE OF OUTDOOR RELIEF DEPARTMENTS AND OF ALL GENERAL DEPARTMENTS

16 Cities, 1911–1931

Note: Broken lines indicate data not available or not available in comparable form for these years.

Source: U. S. Department of Commerce, Bureau of the Census, annual reports, *Financial Statistics of Cities Having a Population of Over 100,000, 1911–1931.*

AF-1349, W. P. A.

[21] See p. 12 ff.

payments for the support of all general departments of government [22] and increased out of all proportion to population growth. Whereas population in the 16 cities increased 45 percent, governmental-cost payments for all general departments [23] increased 300 percent and for relief more than 4,000 percent.

Table 4.—Population and Governmental-Cost Payments for Operation and Maintenance of All General Departments and of Outdoor Relief Departments in 16 Cities, 1911, 1929, and 1931

Item	1911	1929	1931	Percent increase	
				1911 to 1929	1911 to 1931
	Figures in thousands				
Population	15,032	21,120	21,821	41	45
All general departments	$303,166	$1,080,191	$1,220,412	256	303
Outdoor relief	1,559	18,989	64,142	1,118	4,014
Outdoor care of poor [1]	1,042	6,733	42,998	546	4,026
Aid to soldiers and sailors	503	1,713	6,093	241	1,111
Aid to mothers	14	10,543	15,051	†	†

†Percent increase not computed because of smallness of base.

[1] Includes aid to the aged and aid to the blind where given.

Trends in Relief Expenditures in 36 Large Cities, 1916–1925

The long-time view of public relief trends afforded by the data on governmental-cost payments for the 21 years ending in 1931 cannot be matched by similar comprehensive records of private relief or of total public and private relief expenditures for the period. But further knowledge of past trends is afforded by data for a group of selected agencies in 36 large cities for the 10 years from 1916 through 1925. The data, the results of a study made in 1926 by Ralph G. Hurlin,[24] of the Russell Sage Foundation, serve the further valuable purpose of telling what happened to urban relief expenditures during the depression of 1921–1922, when the census compilations are not available. This study represents the first attempt to develop trends in the field of outdoor relief. Reports on relief expenditures were obtained from selected public and private agencies in 35 of the 68 cities in the United States having populations in 1920 of more than 100,000.[25] With the exception of Los Angeles, these included the 10 largest cities: New York, Chicago, Philadelphia, Detroit, Cleveland, St. Louis, Boston, Baltimore, and Pittsburgh.

[22] Although not necessarily more rapidly than for some individual departments.

[23] Operation and maintenance only; excludes capital outlays and interest.

[24] Hurlin, Ralph G., "The Mounting Bill for Relief," *The Survey*, Vol. LVII, No. 4, November 15, 1926, pp. 207–209.

[25] Harrisburg, Pennsylvania, with a population of 75,000 was the other city included in the study.

The relief expenditures for 96 agencies show a distinct upward trend over the 10-year period. The accompanying diagram, reproduced from Mr. Hurlin's article, compares this upward movement with changes in the cost of living [26] and in population and shows the relief trend adjusted to reflect the influence of these two variables, which necessarily affect relief costs. [27] The 71-percent rise shown by the

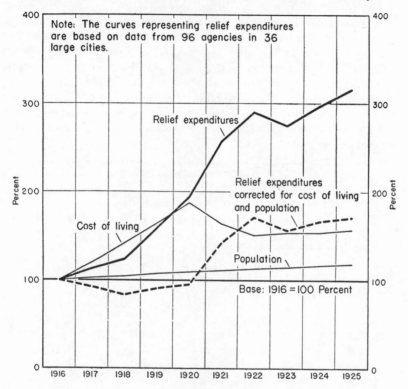

FIG. 2 - RELIEF EXPENDITURES, COST OF LIVING, AND POPULATION

1916 – 1925

Source: Reproduced from Hurlin, Ralph G.,
"The Mounting Bill for Relief," *The Survey*,
Vol. LVII, No. 4, November 15, 1926, pp. 207-209.

AF-1029, W.P.A.

[26] Adjustment made on the basis of the Bureau of Labor Statistics cost of living index.

[27] In order that the curves in fig. 2 might reflect a central tendency in relief expenditures rather than the tendencies of the few largest agencies, the amounts expended by each agency were converted by Mr. Hurlin to relative numbers and averaged for each year.

corrected curve is substantially less than the 215-percent rise of the original. The war-time inflation in living costs accounts for the early dip in the adjusted trend. Both curves register the impact of the 1921–1922 depression. It is significant that relief expenditures did not return to predepression levels after the upswing of the business cycle, and that they resumed an upward trend by 1924.

The trends of aggregate expenditures of 17 public agencies and of 48 private agencies, expressed as relative numbers, are compared in figure 3 with the trend of combined expenditures of these agencies. During the first half of the period the upward trends are almost identical. The depression of 1921–1922 led naturally to increases in expenditures of both groups of agencies, but public expenditures increased at a distinctly more rapid rate than private. This steeper trend of public as compared with private expenditures for relief was not limited to the depression years but was continued and accentuated in subsequent years.

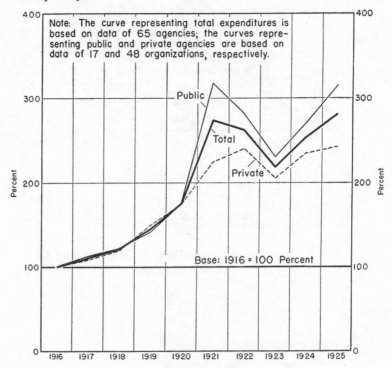

FIG. 3 – RELIEF EXPENDITURES OF PUBLIC AND PRIVATE ORGANIZATIONS

1916 – 1925

Source: Reproduced from Hurlin, Ralph G.,
"The Mounting Bill for Relief," *The Survey*,
Vol. LVII, No. 4, November 15, 1926, pp 207-209.   AF-1031, W.P.A.

Aggregate expenditures for the two groups of agencies were about equal in 1916 and showed a combined increase of 181 percent by 1925. Amounts expended by public agencies increased 215 percent, from $1,685,000 to more than $5,300,000; private expenditures increased 143 percent, from approximately $1,507,000 to $3,661,000.

Rise in Relief Costs in 16 Cities Between 1924 and 1929

An important pathfinding study of the volume and cost of community welfare, made by Raymond Clapp for the year 1924 under the auspices of the American Association of Community Organization, gives further evidence of the long-time rise in relief expenditures. Nineteen cities were included in this survey. For 16 of these—Akron, Buffalo, Canton, Cleveland, Dayton, Des Moines, Detroit, Grand Rapids, Indianapolis, Kansas City (Mo.), Milwaukee, Minneapolis, Omaha, Rochester, St. Paul, and Toledo—comparison can be made of relief expenditures in 1924 with those for the year 1929, as reported to the United States Children's Bureau. The 1924 data cover both private and public outdoor relief, including mothers' aid and blind relief. They may not be entirely comparable with those for recent years,[28] but they are believed to be approximately so and to support the conclusion that there was a general expansion in relief costs be-

Table 5.—Relief Expenditures in 16 Cities, 1924 and 1929

City	Territory included [1]	Source of data		Percent increase, 1924 to 1929 [3]
		Raymond Clapp [2]	U. S. Children's Bureau	
		1924	1929	
		Amount in thousands		
Akron	County	$138	$181	31
Buffalo	County	739	1,415	91
Canton	County	65	152	134
Cleveland	County	741	1,179	59
Dayton	County	103	225	118
Des Moines	County	142	161	13
Detroit	County	1,183	3,040	157
Grand Rapids	County	107	130	21
Indianapolis	County	128	255	99
Kansas City	City	158	231	46
Milwaukee	County	354	686	94
Minneapolis	City	306	422	38
Omaha	County	101	181	79
Rochester	City	342	855	150
St. Paul	County	335	394	18
Toledo	County	121	220	82

[1] These are the territories included in the Children's Bureau Series; the Clapp data represented all agencies operating in the city, which include county agencies.
[2] Clapp, Raymond, "Relief in 19 Cities," *The Survey*, Vol. LVII, No. 4, November 15, 1926, pp. 209–210.
[3] Since the 2 sets of data are not completely comparable these percentages should be interpreted as an approximate measure of the actual change between the 2 dates.

[28] The data for 1924 were collected for a particular study and were not the result of a continuous reporting system which offers an opportunity for subsequent refinement and check.

tween 1924 and 1929 which antedated the rise to present depression levels.

Every one of the 16 cities showed marked increases in expenditures during the interval from 1924 to 1929. In six of the cities the burden increased less than 50 percent, in six others from 50 to 100 percent, and in the remaining four from 100 to 160 percent. The median increase for the group was approximately 80 percent.

Outdoor Relief Expenditures in New Haven, 1910–1925

A prevailing upward trend in outdoor relief expenditures in the city of New Haven (Conn.) for the 26 years extending from 1900 through 1925 is revealed by data compiled in 1928 by Willford I. King.[29] The course of relief expenditures of both public and private agencies during the period 1910 through 1925 is shown in figure 4.[30] The curves in figure 4a represent actual expenditures, inclusive of administrative cost; those in figure 4b reflect adjustment for population growth and conversion to 1913 dollars.[31]

Private agencies bore a heavy share of the relief burden in New Haven throughout the 16 years. The introduction of public relief for widowed mothers increased the proportion of public expenditures

Table 6.—Outdoor Relief Expenditures [1] in New Haven, Specified Years, 1910–1925

	1910	1915	1920	1925
Expenditures in thousands [1]				
Total	$66	$69	$168	$290
Public	16	14	51	112
Private	50	55	117	178
Relative numbers of expenditures				
Total	100	105	255	439
Public	100	88	319	700
Private	100	110	234	356
Relative numbers of expenditures per inhabitant in terms of 1913 dollars				
Total	100	92	102	196
Public	100	77	127	310
Private	100	97	94	159

[1] Includes cost of administration.

[29] See King, Willford I., *Trends in Philanthropy*, National Bureau of Economic Research, New York, 1928.

[30] Between 1900 and 1910 there was a mild rise in the expenditures of both public and private agencies.

[31] Population estimates for intercensal years were made by Mr. King. King, Willford I., *op. cit.*, p. 68. An index of prices of direct or consumers' goods was used to reduce actual dollars to dollars of constant purchasing power. See King, pp. 61–62.

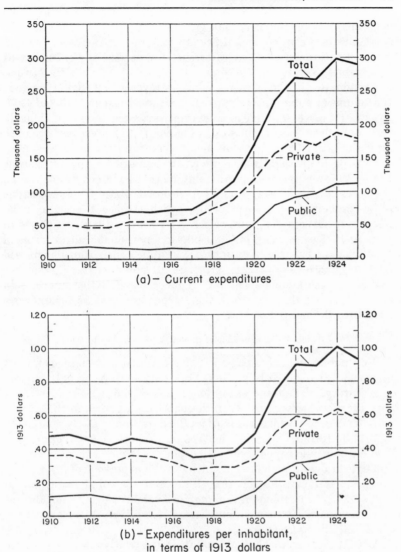

(a)− Current expenditures

(b)−Expenditures per inhabitant,
in terms of 1913 dollars

FIG. 4−OUTDOOR RELIEF EXPENDITURES IN NEW HAVEN

1910−1925

Source: King, Willford I., *Trends in Philanthropy*,
National Bureau of Economic Research, New York, 1928.

AF-1105, W.P.A.

somewhat after 1920 but did not greatly alter the division of the relief
burden as between public and private resources. At 5-year intervals
from 1910 through 1925, private relief comprised 76, 80, 70, and 61
percent, respectively, of the total.

Examination of the curves in figure 4a reveals only slight change in
the volume of public and private expenditures between 1910 and 1917.
After 1917, however, there is an abrupt rise in the volume of expenditures of both types of agencies. A temporary dip downward occurred
after the 1921–1922 depression, but expenditures reached a new peak
in 1924, declining slightly thereafter. In terms of constant purchasing
power, the trend of relief per inhabitant is sharply downward during
the period of the World War. This drop, shown in figure 4b, is due
to the war-time inflation of prices, which reached a peak in 1920.
Total expenditures for outdoor relief were more than four times as
large in 1925 as in 1910, but expenditures per inhabitant in terms of
1913 dollars were less than doubled. Public expenditures increased
relatively more than private, although still representing the smaller
fraction of the annual relief bill in the city. Relative numbers in
table 6 indicate the changes in relief expenditures at 5-year intervals
from 1910 through 1925.

Outdoor Relief Expenditures in New York City, 1910–1934

Both public and private agencies have shared in a marked upward
movement in relief costs in New York City during the past quarter
of a century. The trend of outdoor relief expenditures in New York
City for the 20 years from 1910 through 1929 is shown in the accompanying diagram, which summarizes the data from a study completed
in 1934 by Kate Huntley for the Welfare Council of New York City.[32]
The data include expenditures from both public and private sources
and extend over a period which includes the depression of 1914–1915,
the postwar depression of 1921–1922, and the minor recession of
1927–1928.[33] The trend for the combined volume of relief expenditures
and the separate trends for public and for private relief are shown
graphically in figure 5a.

After 1916 there was a distinct shift in the relative levels of private
and public expenditures. Prior to that year relief expenditures from
public funds were comparatively small and confined to relief for a few
special groups, including veterans and volunteer firemen, and their
families, and the adult blind. In 1916, however, a new State law
provided relief for mothers with dependent children. From that date
there has been steady growth in relief from public funds, and since

---

[32] Huntley, Kate, *Financial Trends in Organized Social Work in New York City*,
Columbia University Press, New York, 1935.

[33] The figures given here exclude expenditures for service and administration
incident to relief.

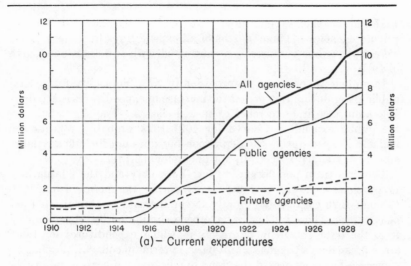

(a)– Current expenditures

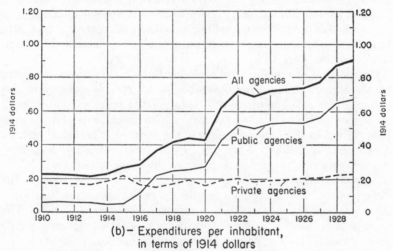

(b)– Expenditures per inhabitant,
in terms of 1914 dollars

FIG. 5– EXPENDITURES FOR OUTDOOR RELIEF FROM
PUBLIC AND PRIVATE RESOURCES
IN NEW YORK CITY

1910 –1929

Source: Fig. 5(a) adapted, and Fig. 5(b) reproduced,
from Huntley, Kate, *Financial Trends in Organized
Social Work in New York City*, Columbia University
Press, New York, 1935, pp. 71, 75.

AF–1035, W.P.A.

1917 public relief expenditures have consistently exceeded those of private agencies. Three-fourths of all expenditures for relief in 1929 were from public resources, as contrasted with less than one-fourth in 1910.

Inasmuch as there was no provision in New York City for general public relief during this period the increase in expenditures is attributable almost entirely to relief to special classes. The slight bulge in the public expenditure curve for 1921–1922 probably reflects the increase in need during the depression but does not include any large amounts extended specifically for unemployment relief.

The growth in population in New York City and the fluctuations in purchasing power of relief funds during the period from 1910 through 1929 contributed greatly to the increase in annual relief expenditures. These influences have been eliminated by Miss Huntley from the data shown in figure 5b, in which expenditures for relief are expressed on a per-inhabitant basis, in terms of constant purchasing power.[34] The steepness of the trend in relief expenditures is materially lessened by this adjustment. Annual expenditures per inhabitant, in terms of 1914 dollars, increased approximately 300 percent from 1910 to 1929, as compared with an increase of 970 percent in actual expenditures for New York City.

Comparison of relief expenditures for these earlier years with data for the 5 years ending with December 1934 [35] reveals a staggering increase in the relief burden since 1929. Total relief expenditures in 1910 were only six-tenths of 1 percent of the expenditures for the year 1934. Even in 1930, the beginning of the depression period, they were only 7 percent of the 1934 amount. In the intervening 3 years annual expenditures rose rapidly in response to the needs of the unemployed.

Strenuous efforts of private organizations to meet the crisis in the early phase of the depression are reflected in the figures for 1931 when there was a sharp increase in the proportions of private funds. The passage of legislation in New York State in 1931 authorizing public relief through the Temporary Emergency Relief Administration, the first State emergency relief organization to be created in the United States, marked the beginning of active public participation in unemployment relief in New York City. Very substantial amounts of relief from private sources were given during the next 2 years, but these amounts represented a rapidly declining proportion of the total.

---

[34] The cost of living index used to correct relief expenditures was derived from the Bureau of Labor Statistics index of the cost of living in New York City after 1914, and earlier data on retail prices of food for the North Atlantic Division collected by the Department of Labor. The indices were revised by Miss Huntley to accord more weight to food and rent, which are relatively more important in a relief budget. See Huntley, Kate, op. cit., Appendix III for a full description of the index used.

[35] These data were collected by Miss Huntley for the Welfare Council of New York City and are entirely comparable with those for earlier years.

It should be noted that even without any statutory provision for public outdoor poor relief, public resources supplied the major portion of relief funds in New York City for at least 14 years [36] before the establishment of an emergency unemployment relief program. Since 1933 public resources have borne a preponderant share of the total relief bill. Private agencies accounted for only 4 percent of the total in 1934. The long-time shifts in the relative amounts of public and private funds for relief purposes are shown clearly in table 7.

Table 7.—Expenditures for Outdoor Relief [1] From Public and Private Resources, New York City, Specified Years, 1910–1934

Year [2]	Amount in thousands			Percent		Total as percent of 1934
	Total [3]	Public resources	Private resources	Public resources	Private resources	
1910	$971	$229	$743	23. 6	76. 4	0. 6
1915	1, 395	256	1, 139	18. 4	81. 6	0. 8
1920	4, 750	2, 981	1, 769	62. 8	37. 2	2. 7
1925	7, 729	5, 662	2, 068	73. 3	26. 7	4. 4
1929	10, 387	7, 750	2, 637	74. 6	25. 4	5. 9
1930	12, 926	9, 271	3, 654	71. 7	28. 3	7. 3
1931	48, 164	31, 665	16, 499	65. 7	34. 3	27. 3
1932	82, 366	57, 870	24, 496	70. 3	29. 7	46. 7
1933	[4] 118, 361	[4] 101, 211	17, 151	85. 5	14. 5	67. 1
1934	[4] 176, 514	[4] 169, 316	7, 198	95. 9	4. 1	100. 0

[1] Expenditures for administration excluded except as indicated in footnote 4 below.
[2] Data for 1910 through 1929 from Huntley, *Financial Trends in Organized Social Work in New York City* those for 1930 through 1934 supplied in unpublished form by the Welfare Council of New York City.
[3] Derived from data carried to more places; therefore, differs slightly from sum of items.
[4] Includes payments to those workers who received relief wages on staffs of relief projects. Does not include wages paid for CWA employment, which totaled $8,751,000 in 1933 and $34,467,000 in 1934.

Expenditures for Public Outdoor Relief in New York State, 1910–1934

Data on expenditures for public outdoor relief in New York State, compiled and made available by the State Department of Social Welfare,[37] show a gradual expansion in relief costs for 20 years before the precipitous rise beginning in 1930. The data, which are exclusive of administrative costs, represent expenditures for home (direct) relief, including aid to veterans; for work relief; and for three types of categorical relief—aid to the aged, aid to the blind, and aid to dependent children.[38] The figures do not include expenditures of the Civil Works Administration, which made wage payments in New York State in 1933 of more than $14,000,000 and in 1934 of more than

[36] See fig. 5a.

[37] Supplied in unpublished form. Data for 1910 through 1915 for fiscal years ending September 30; for 1916, 9 months ending June 30; for 1917–1934, fiscal years ending June 30.

[38] Reimbursable expenditures for relief incurred by private agencies for public charges are included. Expenditures for the years 1932–1934 for home and work relief represent commitments made by the Temporary Emergency Relief Administration of New York State and hence do not cover some small amounts of local relief not reimbursable from State funds.

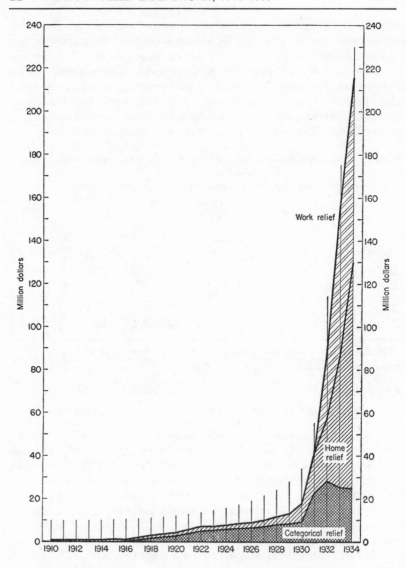

FIG. 6–EXPENDITURES FOR PUBLIC OUTDOOR RELIEF
NEW YORK STATE
1910–1934

Source: New York State, Department of
Social Welfare, unpublished data.

AF-1471, W.P.A.

$60,000,000. The combined volume of expenditures for home (direct) relief, work relief, and categorical relief over the 25-year period are shown in figure 6.

Between 1910 and 1916 little change in the total amount of relief is recorded, but after 1916 expenditures mount substantially, increasing gradually until 1931 when there is an extremely sharp rise which continues during the next 3 years. The introduction of child welfare allowances in 1916 and of aid to the aged in 1931 accounts for the expansion in categorical assistance. The startling increase in home relief and the inauguration of work relief followed the creation of the New York Temporary Emergency Relief Administration in 1931.

The rising relief costs, even before 1930, were due only in small part to the growth of population in New York State. Total expenditures rose from $885,000 in 1910 to $17,786,000 in 1930 and $215,601,000 in 1934, while expenditures per inhabitant rose from $0.10 in 1910 to $1.41 and $16.51 in 1930 and 1934, respectively. Actual expenditures for the several classes of relief and expenditures per inhabitant at 5-year intervals from 1910 through 1930 and for the year 1934 are shown in table 8.

Table 8.—Expenditures for Public Outdoor Relief in New York State, Specified Years, 1910–1934 [1]

Year	Total	General relief		Categorical assistance		
		Home relief [2]	Work relief	Aid to the aged	Aid to the blind	Aid to dependent children
Amount in thousands						
1910	$885	$830	—	—	$55	—
1915	1,277	1,222	—	—	55	—
1920	4,351	1,457	—	—	66	$2,828
1925	8,548	2,184	—	—	209	6,154
1930	17,786	8,517	—	—	323	8,946
1934	215,601	104,921	$85,638	$12,651	372	12,019
Amount per inhabitant [3]						
1910	$0.10	$0.09	—	—	$0.01	—
1915	.13	.12	—	—	.01	—
1920	.41	.13	—	—	.01	$0.27
1925	.74	.19	—	—	.02	.53
1930	1.41	.67	—	—	.03	.71
1934	16.51	8.03	$6.55	$0.97	.03	.92

[1] Data for 1910 and 1915 are for fiscal years ending September 30; data for other years are for fiscal years ending June 30.
[2] Includes veteran relief.
[3] U. S. Bureau of the Census annual State population estimates used; computed from unrounded data.

Expenditures for Public Outdoor Poor Relief in Indiana, 1910–1931

Annual expenditures for public outdoor poor relief in Indiana show that this State shared in the general rise in public relief costs after

1910. These data were compiled by the Indiana State Board of Charities from quarterly reports of township officials for the years from 1890 through 1931, and they were presented graphically in a recent report of the Governor's Commission on Unemployment Relief.[39] Analysis here is confined to the years 1910 through 1931, which come within the scope of this report.[40]

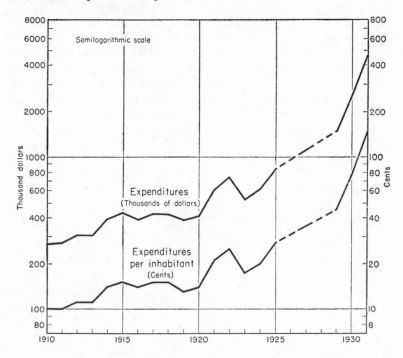

FIG. 7 – EXPENDITURES FOR PUBLIC OUTDOOR POOR
RELIEF IN INDIANA
1910 – 1931

Note. Broken lines indicate data not available or not available in comparable form for these years.

Source: State of Indiana, Governor's Commission on Unemployment Relief, *Year Book April 1933 – June 1934, July 1934 – June 1935*

AF–1461, W.P.A.

---

[39] State of Indiana, Governor's Commission on Unemployment Relief, *Year Book, April 1933–June 1934, July 1934–June 1935*, pp. 3–9.

[40] Between 1890 and 1895 expenditures for outdoor relief were at a higher level than in any subsequent year until 1921. In 1890, the first year for which data are available, public expenditures for outdoor poor relief totaled $560,000. By 1895 they had risen to $630,000. Thereafter there was a progressive decline, the level of expenditures between 1900 and 1910 being somewhat below that in the next decade.

The annual amounts expended for outdoor poor relief increased from $266,000 in 1910 to $4,681,000 in 1931, while expenditures per inhabitant rose from $0.10 to $1.44. Expenditures in selected years beginning with 1910 are given in table 9. The data are exclusive of administrative costs and represent all outdoor relief granted from public funds, except public assistance to the blind and to mothers with dependent children.

Rates of increase in annual expenditures and in expenditures per inhabitant, compared in figure 7, have been very similar. The two curves, plotted on a semilogarithmic or ratio scale, reveal a considerable increase in the rate of expansion in expenditures during the 1914–1915 and the 1921–1922 depressions, and a very sharp expansion during the depression years of 1930 and 1931.

Table 9.—Expenditures for Public Outdoor Poor Relief [1] in Indiana, Specified Years, 1910–1931

Year	Amount in thousands	Amount per inhabitant [1]	Year	Amount in thousands	Amount per inhabitant [1]
1910	$266	$0.10	1925	$841	$0.27
1915	435	.15	1930	2,506	.77
1920	417	.14	1931	4,681	1.44

[1] U. S. Bureau of the Census State estimates of population used to compute expenditures per inhabitant.

Following the 1914–1915 depression there was almost no decline in annual expenditures. The failure of expenditures to contract after the revival of business is doubtless due in part to the decline in the purchasing power of the dollar during the World War. Immediately after the 1921–1922 depression there was a drop from the peak, but this drop was followed immediately by a marked upward movement which continued and was greatly accelerated at the onset of the depression in 1930 and 1931.

THE RISE IN RELIEF EXPENDITURES SINCE 1929

Expansion in Urban Relief Between 1929 and 1931

Until the current depression the gradual rise in relief costs over the years was a matter for State and local rather than national concern. But with the advent of the depression, relief costs throughout the country moved rapidly upward, overtaxing local and State resources and thus focusing attention on the Nation-wide problems of unemployment and the relief of distress caused by unemployment. This abrupt change in the scope and focus of the relief problem suggests the need for a review of relief expenditures since 1929, the last year of comparatively "normal" relief costs.

The first attempt to collect statistics of the volume of relief on a Nation-wide basis was made by the United States Bureau of the

Census [41] during the summer of 1931 at the request of the President's Organization on Unemployment Relief. As the depression grew more acute and demands for relief increased sharply with decreasing employment, need for such Nation-wide measurement of the relief problem had become evident.

Information indicating the amounts of relief disbursed by public and private agencies to families in their homes and to homeless men [42] during the first quarters of 1929 and 1931 was collected and tabulated separately for 308 cities of over 30,000 population, and for counties and smaller incorporated places.[43] Administrative expense was included in the figures for some agencies but not for all so that the amounts given understate for both periods the total expenditures for relief and its administration.[44] It is important to realize that the first quarter of the year normally represents a seasonal peak in relief operations and hence expenditures in the first quarter of 1929 were probably somewhat larger than those for the other quarters of the year. In 1931, however, the growing severity of the unemployment crisis may have more than counterbalanced the seasonal factor, leading to higher expenditures in subsequent quarters of the year. Since returns from the counties and smaller incorporated places were incomplete, discussion here is confined to the 308 cities grouped by States and by geographic divisions.

Country-wide expansion in urban relief expenditures between the two periods is shown by the figures for different geographic divisions, given in table 10. The combined expenditures of the cities in these nine divisions rose 241 percent between the first quarter of 1929 and the first quarter of 1931, or from $16,621,000 to $56,669,000. Governmental relief expenditures increased 217 percent and private expenditures 286 percent. Individual State aggregates are given in appendix table 2.

Striking variations are evident both in the amount of relief disbursed and in the degree of expansion in relief in the different geographic divisions. These variations reflect in part at least the promptness

---

[41] The U. S. Children's Bureau and the Russell Sage Foundation cooperated in the survey, obtaining data for cities over 30,000 population through previously-established reporting contacts. Reports for expenditures for relief in cities having less than 30,000 population and for county governments were obtained by the Census Bureau chiefly through correspondence with postmasters and county officials.

[42] Includes relief to special classes as well as direct and work relief.

[43] Returns were received from 308 of the 310 cities having 30,000 or more inhabitants in 1930. No returns were received from Santa Ana, Calif., or from Pawtucket, R. I. Six States, Idaho, Nevada, New Mexico, North Dakota, Vermont, and Wyoming, contain no cities of 30,000 or more inhabitants.

[44] It was intended that administrative costs be included in every instance, but for many agencies it was not possible to segregate the cost of administering relief from other administrative functions, so that only the amount of relief granted was reported.

Table 10.—Expenditures for Relief to Families in Their Homes and to Homeless Men in 308 Cities,[1] by Geographic Division, First Quarters of 1929 and of 1931

Cities in geographic division of over 30,000 population	Number of cities	Amount in thousands [2]		Percent of increase from 1929 to 1931
		First quarter of 1929	First quarter of 1931	
Total expenditures				
All divisions	308	$16,621	$56,669	241
New England	44	3,100	7,585	145
Middle Atlantic	64	5,612	21,250	279
East North Central	81	3,878	17,935	363
West North Central	21	1,142	2,219	94
South Atlantic	34	587	1,407	140
East South Central	13	214	698	226
West South Central	21	281	866	209
Mountain	8	269	447	66
Pacific	22	1,539	4,265	177
Governmental expenditures				
All divisions	308	$10,802	$34,201	217
New England	44	2,532	6,569	160
Middle Atlantic	64	3,798	9,819	159
East North Central	81	2,559	12,252	379
West North Central	21	565	1,101	95
South Atlantic	34	159	364	128
East South Central	13	40	274	589
West South Central	21	87	392	352
Mountain	8	193	304	57
Pacific	22	869	3,126	260
Private expenditures				
All divisions	308	$5,819	$22,468	286
New England	44	568	1,015	79
Middle Atlantic	64	1,814	11,431	530
East North Central	81	1,318	5,683	331
West North Central	21	577	1,118	94
South Atlantic	34	428	1,043	144
East South Central	13	174	422	142
West South Central	21	194	474	145
Mountain	8	76	144	89
Pacific	22	670	1,138	70

[1] Cities with a population of over 30,000.
[2] Since figures are rounded to the nearest thousand, totals will not in all cases equal the sum of the parts.

Source: U. S. Department of Commerce, Bureau of the Census, special report, *Relief Expenditures by Governmental and Private Organizations, 1929 and 1931*, 1932.

and force with which the cities in these different areas felt the impact of the depression and the extent to which organized relief met the ensuing distress. But it should be remembered that percentage change is definitely affected by the amount of city relief expenditures in the several areas in the 1929 predepression base period. A relatively small percentage increase in expenditures may reflect a relatively high standard of care in 1929 rather than failure to meet increasing relief needs in 1931. This is definitely the situation in the cities in the New England Area, which registered an increase of 145 percent in total relief expenditures as compared with a 241 percent increase for the combined areas. Expenditures per inhabitant in the New

England cities were, as indicated in table 11, more than double those in other areas in the 1929 quarter, with the exception of the Mountain Area.

Table 11.—Expenditures per Inhabitant for Relief to Families in Their Homes and to Homeless Men in 308 Cities,[1] by Geographic Division, First Quarters of 1929 and of 1931

Geographic division	Number of cities	First quarter of 1929	First quarter of 1931
All divisions	308	$0.34	$1.17
New England	44	.75	1.85
Middle Atlantic	64	.36	1.37
East North Central	81	.31	1.43
West North Central	21	.34	.67
South Atlantic	34	.16	.39
East South Central	13	.14	.45
West South Central	21	.11	.35
Mountain	8	.40	.67
Pacific	22	.33	.91

[1] Cities with a population of over 30,000.

Wide range in the ratio of governmental relief expenditures to total expenditures for relief appears from the data for geographic divisions and for the individual States.[45]   While the proportion of governmental expenditures in all cities combined declined only slightly between the two quarters, from 65 to 60 percent, there was significant decline in the Middle Atlantic States, which were particularly active in the provision of unemployment relief through private emergency organizations.   A marked rise in the proportion of public relief is recorded in the East South Central, West South Central, and Pacific Divisions. During the first quarter of 1929 public relief constituted less than 25 percent of the total city relief in 11 States [46] and more than 75 percent in 8 States; governmental expenditures were from 25 to 75 percent of the total in 23 States and the District of Columbia.

Table 12.—Governmental Relief Expenditures as Percent of Total Expenditures for Relief to Families in Their Homes and to Homeless Men in 308 Cities,[1] by Geographic Division, First Quarters of 1929 and of 1931

Geographic division	Number of cities	First quarter of 1929	First quarter of 1931
All divisions	308	65.0	60.4
New England	44	81.7	86.6
Middle Atlantic	64	67.7	46.2
East North Central	81	66.0	68.3
West North Central	21	49.5	49.6
South Atlantic	34	27.2	25.8
East South Central	13	18.6	39.4
West South Central	21	30.9	45.3
Mountain	8	71.8	67.8
Pacific	22	56.5	73.3

[1] Cities with a population of over 30,000.

[45] See table 12 and appendix table 2.

[46] Cities in two of these States, Alabama and Delaware, reported no public relief in 1929.

Relief Expenditures in 120 Urban Areas, 1929–1935

An invaluable record of urban relief trends prior to the period of Federal participation in relief is afforded by the Urban Relief Series of the U. S. Children's Bureau, which supplies continuous monthly data on relief expenditures from public and private funds in 120 major city areas from January 1929.[47]   Not only does this series provide the connecting link for the 34 months between the onset of the depression and the inauguration of Federal relief but it includes some 9 months of "prosperity" preceding the stock market crash in October 1929.   It also affords the opportunity for seeing the Federal relief program in relation to the relief operations of other public and private agencies. Inasmuch as important shifts in emphasis on different types of relief and on various sources of relief funds have taken place in the past several years, and are likely to continue to take place in the future, particular value is attached to this series, which gives a picture of the over-all relief situation in these urban areas.   The series does not include wage assistance extended through the work programs discussed in Part II of this report.[48]

The urban areas represented in the series include 99 cities with populations of over 100,000 in 1930, and 21 cities with populations between 50,000 and 100,000.   They represent two-thirds of the total urban and somewhat more than one-third of the total population of the United States.   The cities are listed in appendix table 4.

A graphic record of the major changes which have occurred in relief expenditures for these urban areas during the past 7 years is given by the series of diagrams presented in this section.   Major changes in the relative importance of private relief, general public relief, and special allowances [49] appear in figure 8, which shows the monthly relief expenditures for all cities and the variations in the three main classes of relief during the period from 1929 through 1935.   The annual

---

[47] These data are exclusive of administrative cost.   The Urban Relief Series was initiated in 1929 by the Russell Sage Foundation which built up a collection of monthly data for relief agencies in 76 U. S. cities and 5 Canadian cities with populations over 100,000.   This series was transferred as of January 1932 to the U. S. Children's Bureau and was expanded to include other urban areas, mostly between 50,000 and 100,000 in population, for some of which monthly statistics on relief and transient care had been compiled since late in 1930 by the Children's Bureau at the request of the President's Organization on Unemployment Relief, or which had been collected in connection with the Bureau's project for the collection of Social Statistics in Registration Areas.   The Urban Relief Series was transferred to the Social Security Board as of July 1936.

[48] Omitted are the Civil Works Program, the Works Program, and special programs administered by the FERA, including the emergency education, college student aid, rural rehabilitation, and transient programs.

[49] Special allowances include expenditures made under State laws authorizing grants from public funds for mothers' aid, old-age assistance, and aid to the blind. The term is synonymous with public categorical relief, as used in this report. See footnote 3, p. 2.

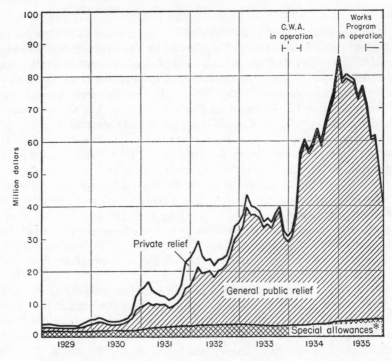

FIG. 8 - TREND OF RELIEF EXPENDITURES FROM PUBLIC
AND PRIVATE FUNDS
IN 120 URBAN AREAS
1929-1935

* Includes aid to the aged, aid to the blind,
and aid to dependent children.

Source: Winslow, Emma A., *Trends in Different
Types of Public and Private Relief in Urban
Areas, 1929–35*, Publication 237, U. S.
Department of Labor, Children's Bureau, 1937.

AF-1365, W. P. A.

expenditures and percentage distributions by class of relief are given
in table 13. Monthly expenditures for the various types of relief,
expressed as relative numbers, are shown in appendix table 5.[50]

The group of private relief agencies is comprised of nonsectarian
family societies, Protestant, Catholic, and Jewish family organizations,
emergency relief agencies under private auspices, and a number of
miscellaneous organizations giving relatively small amounts of outdoor

---

[50] These relative numbers were constructed for this report. For absolute
amounts, see Winslow, Emma A., *Trends in Different Types of Public and Private
Relief in Urban Areas, 1929–35*, Publication No. 237, U. S. Department of Labor,
Children's Bureau, 1937, appendix table A, p. 69.

relief to families in their homes. The American Red Cross and the Salvation Army are in this last group.[51] Agencies giving general public relief include local poor relief offices, public welfare departments, public veteran relief organizations, and local emergency relief administrations. Agencies extending special allowances are those offices or bureaus administering public aid to the aged, to the blind, and to dependent children.[52]

Table 13.—Expenditures for Relief From Public and Private Funds in 120 Urban Areas, 1929–1935

| Year | Grand total | Public funds | | | Private funds |
		Total	General	Special allowances	
	Amount in thousands				
Total, 7 years	$2, 553, 045	$2, 365, 350	$2, 104, 509	$260, 841	$187, 695
1929	43, 745	33, 449	14, 853	18, 596	10, 296
1930	71, 425	54, 754	33, 510	21, 244	16, 671
1931	172, 749	123, 320	88, 594	34, 726	49, 429
1932	308, 185	251, 104	208, 694	42, 410	57, 081
1933	[1] 448, 921	[1] 421, 032	[1] 379, 722	41, 310	27, 889
1934	[1] 667, 153	[1] 652, 467	[1] 608, 880	43, 587	14, 686
1935	[2] 840, 867	[2] 829, 224	[2] 770, 256	58, 968	11, 643
	Percent distribution [3]				
Total, 7 years	100. 0	92. 6	82. 4	10. 2	7. 4
1929	100. 0	76. 5	34. 0	42. 5	23. 5
1930	100. 0	76. 7	46. 9	29. 8	23. 3
1931	100. 0	71. 4	51. 3	20. 1	28. 6
1932	100. 0	81. 5	67. 7	13. 8	18. 5
1933	[1] 100. 0	[1] 93. 8	[1] 84. 6	9. 2	6. 2
1934	[1] 100. 0	[1] 97. 8	[1] 91. 3	6. 5	2. 2
1935	[2] 100. 0	[2] 98. 6	[2] 91. 6	7. 0	1. 4

[1] Excludes expenditures under the Civil Works Administration.
[2] Excludes expenditures under the Works Program.
[3] Computed from unrounded data.

General Rise in Urban Relief

The total relief bill for the 120 cities for the 7-year period was more than $2,553,000,000. Combined annual expenditures mounted from the 1929 low of $44,000,000 to the present all-time high of more than $840,000,000 in 1935. It is significant to note that although 1932 represented the lowest ebb in business activity during the depression, expenditures for relief in these urban areas have more than doubled since that year.[53]

[51] Disaster relief administered by the American Red Cross is not included.

[52] Statutory aid to veterans is classified with general public relief and not with special allowances. Prior to 1934 the Children's Bureau maintained a separate classification for veteran relief, but has not found it feasible to segregate the data for 1934 and 1935. For purposes of consistency, data for veteran relief have in this report been included in general public relief for the entire period.

[53] It should be remembered that these data do not include wage assistance. For a discussion of the trend of relief and wage assistance combined, see Part II.

In 1929, which may be deemed a year of comparatively normal relief expenditures, special allowances, or public categorical relief, constituted 42 percent of the relief bill for these urban areas. General public relief constituted 34 percent and private relief 24 percent of the $44,000,000 total. By 1935 these proportions had shifted extensively, with general public relief forming 92 percent of the vastly larger relief bill. Special allowances and private relief represented only 7 percent and 1 percent, respectively, of the total expenditures for the year. The percentage distribution of relief expenditures for each of the 7 years is shown in figure 9.

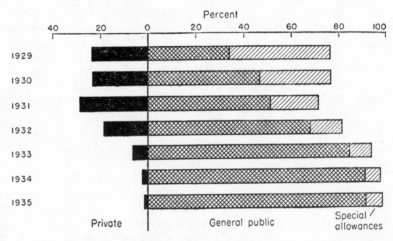

FIG. 9—PERCENT DISTRIBUTION*OF RELIEF EXPENDITURES
FROM PUBLIC AND PRIVATE FUNDS
IN 120 URBAN AREAS

1929-1935

*Each bar totals 100 percent.

Source: Winslow, Emma A., *Trends in Different Types of Public and Private Relief in Urban Areas, 1929-35*, Publication 237, U.S. Department of Labor, Children's Bureau, 1937.

AF-1043, W.P.A.

The important role played by the private agencies in the winters of 1930–1931 and 1931–1932 is apparent. Existing private agencies and newly-created emergency committees made a substantial effort to meet the increasing relief needs but the voluntary contributions collected in emergency relief drives were expended over comparatively short periods of time, resulting in marked fluctuations in the volume of private relief. During this same period expenditures by general public relief agencies increased significantly, but the most startling rise in this type of relief occurred after July 1932, when the Reconstruction Finance Corporation was authorized by the Emergency

Relief and Construction Act to make loans to the States and local subdivisions for relief purposes.[54] Resources liberated by this and subsequent acts [55] made possible the tremendous growth in public disbursement during the second half of the 7-year period.

Relative Proportions of General Public and Private Relief

The interplay of public and private efforts to meet the emergency relief needs is thrown into bold relief by the series of relative numbers plotted in figure 10. These relatives were computed on a base of average monthly expenditures for the 3 years 1931–1933 equaling 100. The curve for public relief excludes special allowances, since these forms of assistance are not primarily intended for families whose dependency is due to unemployment. The expansion of private contributions during two successive winters of voluntary relief drives contrasts sharply with the decline in those contributions after the assumption of responsibility by the Federal Government. This decline must be attributed in part to the exhaustion of private resources as well as to a diminution of private initiative after public funds became available. Even more spectacular than the slump in private expenditures is the concomitant rise in expenditures for general public relief.

Both general public and private relief reflect the seasonal peak in expenditures during the first quarter of the year. Statutory relief through special allowances shows no such seasonal variation, since it is usually given in the form of regular monthly payments.[56]

The relative numbers for January expenditures in each of the 7 years [57] show that private relief rose abruptly from 26 in 1929 to a peak of 233 in January 1932, and had by January 1935 fallen to 31. General public relief rose from 7 in January 1929 to a peak of 427 in January 1935. This peak in general public expenditures coincided with the 7-year peak in total relief expenditures for these areas.

As might be expected, the expansion in the general public relief burden for these 120 urban areas was due almost entirely to the increase in assistance for the unemployed. Public emergency relief was distributed by local poor relief offices, departments of public welfare, emergency commissions, and relief administrations, and after July 1932 was composed in part of Federal funds. Expenditures by emergency

---

[54] By congressional action on June 18, 1934, States were relieved of any obligation to repay loans made under this Act. Hence, Federal participation in relief truly dates from the first loan from RFC funds. Loans made to local subdivisions have not been waived.

[55] Federal Emergency Relief Act of 1933; National Industrial Recovery Act; Act of February 15, 1934; Emergency Appropriation Act, Fiscal Year 1935; Emergency Relief Appropriation Act of 1935.

[56] See fig. 8.

[57] Relative numbers for the 84 months are given in appendix table 5.

relief administrations comprised from 97 to 99 percent of total general public relief during the months from September 1933 through December 1935.[58] The proportion of emergency relief funds dropped during the CWA program and began to decline again with the introduction of the Works Program and the withdrawal of the Federal Government from direct relief in the latter part of 1935.

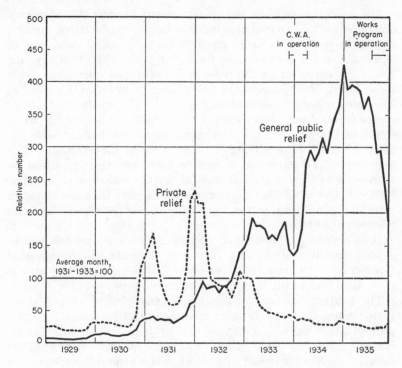

FIG. 10 – EXPENDITURES FOR GENERAL PUBLIC RELIEF AND
FOR PRIVATE RELIEF IN 120 URBAN AREAS,
EXPRESSED AS RELATIVE NUMBERS

1929 – 1935

Source: Winslow, Emma A., *Trends in Different
Types of Public and Private Relief in Urban Areas,
1929-35,* Publication 237, U.S. Department of
Labor, Children's Bureau, 1937   AF–1363, W.P.A.

[58] See U. S. Department of Labor, Children's Bureau, monthly bulletins, *Changes in Different Types of Public and Private Relief in Urban Areas.* Expenditures "reported to FERA" include in some instances small amounts of local public relief not administered by the Emergency Relief Administration.

Table 14.—Expenditures for Relief From Public and Private Funds in 120 Urban Areas, Expressed as Relative Numbers, January 1929–January 1935

[Average month 1931–1933=100]

| Month and year | Total | Public | | Private |
		General	Special allowances	
January 1929	14.9	7.1	46.5	26.3
January 1930	20.0	12.4	50.3	31.8
January 1931	55.6	37.2	72.7	132.9
January 1932	93.8	64.4	103.5	233.4
January 1933	135.1	146.2	111.6	100.3
January 1934	118.3	136.1	104.6	40.8
January 1935	332.8	426.9	136.7	31.4

Rise in Special Allowances

The three types of special allowances responded only mildly to the emergency situation created by widespread unemployment. This is apparent from table 15, which gives annual expenditures for aid to the aged, aid to the blind, and aid to dependent children. These forms of relief are designed to aid classes with specific handicaps not directly connected with unemployment. Because of their legal eligibility requirements and financial limitations they are relatively inflexible to depression need. There is some evidence, however, that increasing need during the depression served as an impetus both to enactment of new legislation and to expansion of case loads for these statutory forms

Table 15.—Expenditures for Special Allowances in 120 Urban Areas, by Type of Assistance, 1929–1935

Year	Total	Aid to the aged	Aid to the blind	Aid to dependent children
Amount in thousands				
Total, 7 years	$260,841	$89,477	$17,864	$153,500
1929	18,596	9	1,514	17,073
1930	21,244	1,060	1,912	18,272
1931	34,726	10,423	2,196	22,107
1932	42,410	15,652	2,475	24,283
1933	41,310	15,293	2,674	23,343
1934	43,587	16.654	3,193	23,740
1935	58,968	30,386	3,900	24,682
Percent distribution [1]				
Total, 7 years	100.0	34.3	6.9	58.8
1929	100.0	*	8.1	91.8
1930	100.0	5.0	9.0	86.0
1931	100.0	30.0	6.3	63.7
1932	100.0	36.9	5.8	57.3
1933	100.0	37.0	6.5	56.5
1934	100.0	38.2	7.3	54.5
1935	100.0	51.5	6.6	41.9

* Less than 0.05 percent.
[1] Computed from unrounded data.

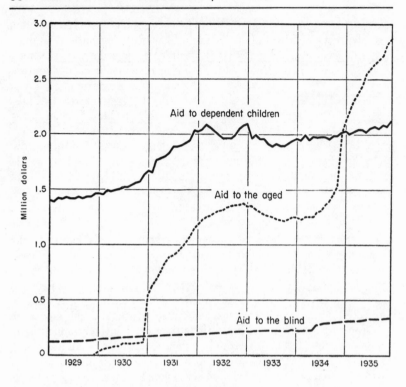

FIG. 11 – EXPENDITURES FOR 3 CATEGORIES OF RELIEF
IN 120 URBAN AREAS
1929 – 1935

Source: Winslow, Emma A., *Trends in Different
Types of Public and Private Relief in Urban
Areas, 1929–35*, Publication 237, U.S.
Department of Labor, Children's Bureau, 1937.   AF-1369, W.P.A.

of relief. The curves in figure 11 show the course of expenditures in
the 120 urban areas for these 3 types of relief.

Aid to the blind increased only slightly at a fairly constant rate over
the 7-year period. The steep rise in the curve for aid to dependent
children may represent, in very slight degree, expansion in the coverage
of existing legislation but suggests also that increasing numbers of
eligibles found it necessary to apply for this type of public relief
because of depleted private resources, or because of the effects of the
depression on relatives or others who had formerly contributed to
their support. The rapid and substantial rise in the amount of old-

age relief is explained largely by the introduction of old-age assistance in several cities under the provisions of new State legislation. Financial difficulties of local and State governments, caused by unprecedented relief burdens combined with declining revenues from tax sources, presumably account for the slump in aid to the aged and in aid to dependent children during 1933 and 1934. Categorical relief did not benefit from Federal grants in these years but was financed solely from State and local funds.[59] Furthermore, there has been no tendency on the part of the States to finance categorical relief by borrowing.[60] Beginning in 1936, however, Federal funds for relief to the aged, to the blind, and to dependent children were made available under the Social Security Act to those States with laws conforming to minimum Federal requirements. As a result, there has been a very sharp expansion in the volume and relative importance of these types of relief since that date.

Relative Proportions of Work and Direct Relief

The relative proportions of general relief distributed in the form of direct and work relief before and during Federal participation in relief activities reflect a growing preference for the latter type of relief for the unemployed. The recent development of work relief as a means of meeting the needs of the destitute unemployed is partially indicated in figure 12, but the omission of the wage assistance programs from the Urban Relief Series tends to obscure the essential continuity of the policy of work projects as a means of assisting the needy unemployed. Thus, the drops in the work relief curve during the winter of 1933–1934 and during the latter part of 1935 do not signify real interruptions in the development of a Federal work relief policy, since the extensive programs of the Civil Works Administration and the Works Program, respectively, were operated on a modified relief basis during these periods.

Work relief was by no means unknown in this country prior to the current depression and was practiced on a small scale as early as the depression of 1914–15,[61] but it was not to be found in the 120

---

[59] FERA Rules and Regulations No. 3, issued July 11, 1933, provided that direct relief should not include relief for widows or their dependents and/or aged persons where provision was already made under existing law. This ruling did not, of course, prevent the extension of general relief to needy persons in these classes when there was no legal provision for categorical relief, or when State or local funds were inadequate to care for all those eligible for these types of assistance.

[60] See Lowe, Robert C., *Analysis of Current State and Local Funds Specifically Assigned to Various Welfare Activities*, Division of Social Research, Works Progress Administration, March 16, 1936.

[61] Colcord, Joanna; Koplovitz, William C.; and Kurtz, Russell H.; *Emergency Work Relief*, Russell Sage Foundation, New York, 1932, p. 12.

cities in significant quantities in 1929 nor in 1930 until the last quarter of the year. There were some small work projects in operation but these were conducted primarily for purposes of administering a "work test" rather than as a means of providing systematic work opportunity to the needy unemployed. Despite the fact that the early work relief figures, for the reason cited, are not strictly comparable with the later figures for work relief under the Federal Emergency Relief Administration,[62] they have value in affording at least a rough measure of the volume of these early work relief projects. The data do not reveal the intermittent character of many of the programs, which were of short duration and predicated on the hope that prosperity and revival of private industry would occur promptly.

Table 16.—Expenditures for General Direct and Work Relief [1] in 120 Urban Areas, 1929–1935

Year	Amount in thousands			Percent [2]	
	Total	Direct	Work	Direct	Work
Total, 7 years	$2,292,204	$1,620,449	$671,755	70.7	29.3
1929	25,149	25,120	29	99.9	0.1
1930	50,181	46,353	3,828	92.4	7.6
1931	138,023	100,866	37,157	73.1	26.9
1932	265,775	199,677	66,098	75.1	24.9
1933	[3] 407,611	295,412	[3] 112,199	72.5	[3] 27.5
1934	[3] 623,566	408,104	[3] 215,462	65.4	[3] 34.6
1935	[4] 781,899	544,917	[4] 236,982	69.7	[4] 30.3

[1] Includes general relief expenditures by both public and private agencies.
[2] Computed from unrounded data.
[3] Excludes expenditures under the Civil Works Administration.
[4] Excludes expenditures under the Works Program.

During 1929 work relief accounted for only one-tenth of 1 percent of relief expenditures in the 120 cities. In 1934 and 1935 approximately one-third of the total relief expenditures were in the form of work relief wages. The annual amounts expended for work relief and for direct relief in the 120 urban areas from 1929 through 1935 and the relative proportions of the two forms of relief are shown in table 16. These proportions do not, of course, convey the full import of the trend toward work and away from direct relief as a means of caring for the able-bodied unemployed, because they do not include amounts expended for either Civil Works Administration or Works Program wages. The influence of these two programs in transferring large numbers from the work relief rolls is evident from the precipitous drops

[62] Instructions for FERA statistical reports were to include as "work relief" only actual work relief projects and not work equivalents (work for relief) or work tests required of recipients of direct relief. Direct relief was synonymous with home relief. See FERA Form 10A General Instructions, Federal Emergency Relief Administration, 1933.

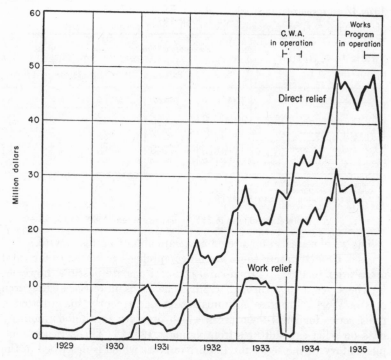

FIG. 12 - EXPENDITURES FROM PUBLIC AND PRIVATE FUNDS
FOR DIRECT RELIEF*AND FOR WORK
RELIEF**IN 120 URBAN AREAS

1929-1935

* Excludes aid to the aged, aid to the blind,
and aid to dependent children.

**Excludes C.W.A., C.C.C., and Works Program.

Source: Winslow, Emma A., *Trends in Different
Types of Public and Private Relief in Urban
Areas, 1929 –35*, Publication 237, U.S.
Department of Labor, Children's Bureau, 1937.

AF ÷1367, W.P.A.

in the work relief curve in figure 12. Their effect on the total relief
burden for the same periods may be seen from figure 8.[63]

Since the introduction of Federal relief and work programs, work
relief sponsored by private agencies has declined to a negligible percentage of the total amount spent for this form of relief. The relative
extent to which private and public relief agencies in these cities
utilized work relief measures during these 7 years is shown in table 17.

[63] Discussion of these work programs, sponsored by the Federal Government
during the second half of the 7-year period, will be given in Part II of this report.

Table 17.—Expenditures for Work Relief From Public and Private Funds in 120 Urban Areas, 1929–1935

Year	Amount in thousands			Percent [1]	
	Total	Public	Private	Public	Private
Total, 7 years	$671,755	$632,629	$39,126	94.2	5.8
1929	29	25	4	86.1	13.9
1930	3,828	1,778	2,050	46.5	53.5
1931	37,157	22,570	14,587	60.7	39.3
1932	66,098	52,051	14,047	78.7	21.3
1933	[2] 112,199	[2] 105,463	6,736	[2] 94.0	6.0
1934	[2] 215,462	[2] 214,281	1,181	[2] 99.5	0.5
1935	[3] 236,982	[3] 236,461	521	[3] 99.8	0.2

[1] Computed from unrounded data.
[2] Excludes expenditures under the Civil Works Administration.
[3] Excludes expenditures under the Works Program.

Relief Expenditures in 385 Rural-Town Areas, 1932–1935

The relief series so far presented relate almost exclusively to urban areas. Unfortunately there are no comprehensive statistics for rural areas prior to 1932. Urban-rural comparisons are possible, however, for the 4 years 1932 through 1935. The Division of Social Research of the Works Progress Administration has recently inaugurated a relief series for rural-town areas which provides continuous monthly data on relief expenditures from January 1932.[64] This series is complementary to the series for 120 urban areas which is described in the preceding section.

The Rural-Town Series includes expenditures for outdoor relief from both public and private sources in 385 representative rural counties and townships in 36 States. Reports cover entire counties in all States except Massachusetts and Connecticut, which are represented by individual townships. Some of the counties and townships have towns and small cities with populations up to 25,000. Together the sample areas contain 11.5 percent of the total rural-town population of the United States.[65]

Types of assistance represented in the series are general and veteran relief; statutory relief to the aged, to the blind, and to dependent children; Resettlement emergency grants;[66] and private relief. Excluded from the Rural-Town Series, as from the Urban Series, are all

[64] The Rural-Town Series was inaugurated in July 1936. Available data on relief expenditures in the sample areas since January 1932 were collected to extend the monthly series back to that date. For 1935 and 1936 data were obtained from areas in 36 States; for 1932, 1933, and 1934 from areas in 24, 26, and 35 States, respectively. The series was projected backward by means of monthly link relatives, bringing the data for the entire period up to a 36-State level.

[65] See appendix B for a map showing the distribution of the sample counties and townships.

[66] Grants made by the Resettlement Administration on an emergency basis to meet the immediate needs of clients.

expenditures for wage assistance extended by the Civil Works Administration and the Works Program agencies and relief disbursed by the Federal Emergency Relief Administration through its special programs. Omitted also are all loans made by the Resettlement Administration.[67]

Table 18.—Expenditures for Outdoor Relief From Public and Private Funds in 385 Rural-Town Areas, 1932–1935

| Year | Total outdoor relief | Public funds | | | | Private funds |
		Total public	General and veteran	The aged, the blind, and dependent children	Resettlement emergency grants	
Amount in thousands						
Total, 4 years	$119,093	$118,183	$108,071	$9,833	$279	$910
1932	10,478	10,223	8,163	2,060	—	255
1933	22,984	22,688	20,737	1,951	—	296
1934	39,835	39,664	37,478	2,186	—	171
1935	45,796	45,608	41,693	3,636	279	188
Percent distribution						
Total, 4 years	100.0	99.2	90.7	8.3	0.2	0.8
1932	100.0	97.6	77.9	19.7	—	2.4
1933	100.0	98.7	90.2	8.5	—	1.3
1934	100.0	99.6	94.1	5.5	—	0.4
1935	100.0	99.6	91.1	7.9	0.6	0.4

Annual expenditures for each class of relief and for all classes combined in the 385 rural-town areas are given in table 18 for the years 1932 through 1935. The table shows also the relative importance of the various classes of assistance in the successive years. Total expenditures for outdoor relief in the 385 rural-town areas amounted to $10,478,000 in 1932 and to $45,796,000 in 1935, an increase of approximately 337 percent. During the same interval total expenditures in the 120 areas represented in the Urban Series rose 172 percent.[68]

In the rural-town areas, as in the urban areas, general public relief, including aid to veterans, was the largest single component of the relief structure. Expenditures for this class of relief in 1932 amounted to $8,163,000 and constituted 78 percent of the total outdoor relief in the 385 counties and townships. In 1935 expenditures for this class of relief totaled $41,693,000 and constituted 91 percent of the grand total.

Throughout the 4-year period private funds contributed a negligible proportion of the relief bill. Even in 1932, when large amounts of

---

[67] Burials, hospitalization, and loans, which are included to a small extent in the data reported for the Urban Series, are not included in the Rural-Town Series. However, the amounts for these items in the Urban Series are small and uniform and do not affect appreciably the trend of that series.

[68] See table 13, p. 31, for data from Urban Relief Series.

private emergency funds were being raised for the relief of unemployment in the cities, private relief constituted less than 2½ percent of the total expenditures in the 385 rural-town areas.

Statutory assistance for the aged, the blind, and dependent children was relatively more important in the rural counties and towns than in the urban areas. While expenditures for these types of relief in 1932 represented 20 percent of the total relief in the 385 rural-town areas, they were but 14 percent of the total in the 120 urban areas. Between 1932 and 1935 expenditures for these special classes rose appreciably in absolute amounts, but they declined substantially in relative importance.

The expansion occurring in the combined expenditures for the three groups was due almost entirely to increase in the amount of old-age assistance. This increase was induced by the enactment of new State laws providing assistance to the needy aged.[69] Annual expenditures for aid to the aged, aid to the blind, and aid to dependent children are given in table 19. Marked shifts in the relative volume of aid to the aged and of aid to dependent children are revealed by the table. A similar but less pronounced shift in emphasis between these two forms of allowances was indicated by the data for urban areas.

Table 19.—Expenditures for Relief to the Aged, the Blind, and Dependent Children in 385 Rural-Town Areas, 1932–1935

Year	Total	Aid to the aged	Aid to the blind	Aid to dependent children
Amount in thousands				
Total, 4 years	$9,833	$4,868	$995	$3,970
1932	2,060	732	229	1,099
1933	1,951	742	241	968
1934	2,186	1,024	267	895
1935	3,636	2,370	258	1,008
Percent distribution				
Total, 4 years	100.0	49.5	10.1	40.4
1932	100.0	35.5	11.1	53.4
1933	100.0	38.0	12.4	49.6
1934	100.0	46.9	12.2	40.9
1935	100.0	65.2	7.1	27.7

Relief Expenditures in Rural and Urban United States, 1932–1935

The establishment of the Rural-Town Relief Series, on a basis comparable to the Urban Relief Series, has made feasible for the first time the construction of a combined Urban and Rural-Town Relief

---

[69] See table 1, p. 3, for number of States enacting legislation during this period to provide this form of assistance.

Series reflecting fluctuations in total public and private outdoor relief expenditures in the United States and permitting direct comparisons of the volume and trend of the various types of relief in rural and in urban areas.

Such a combined relief series has recently been built up by the Division of Social Research on the basis of reported expenditures in the 120 urban and 335 rural-town sample areas. Monthly data for the two relief series were generalized to represent the total urban and total rural-town population in the United States; the resulting urban and rural-town series were combined for each month, by type of assistance, to give estimated monthly expenditures for the whole United States. [70] Monthly indices of the combined expenditure series for total outdoor relief from January 1932 through December 1935 are shown in appendix table 6 together with the indices of the component urban and rural-town series.[71] The indices were originally computed with average monthly expenditures in the fiscal year ending

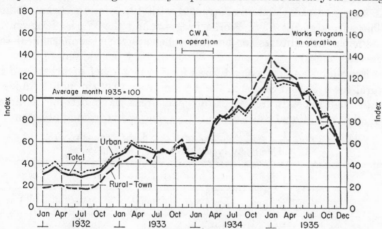

FIG. 13 – TRENDS OF EXPENDITURES FOR OUTDOOR RELIEF
IN RURAL-TOWN AREAS, URBAN AREAS,
AND TOTAL UNITED STATES
January 1932 – December 1935

Source: Division of Social Research, Rural Section,
Works Progress Administration, based on data from
Rural-Town Relief Series and Urban Relief Series.   AF-2223, W.P.A.

[70] For complete description and methodology of the combined series and monthly indices for the component types of relief, see Woofter, T. J., Jr.; Aaronson, Franklin; and Mangus, A. R.: *op. cit.*

[71] The series for urban United States represents counties with cities of 25,000 or over and Connecticut and Massachusetts townships of 5,000 or over; the series for rural-town United States represents counties with no city of 25,000 or over and Massachusetts and Connecticut townships of less than 5,000.

June 1936 equal to 100. For the purpose of this report the indices have been converted to an earlier base, with average monthly expenditures in the calendar year 1935 equal to 100.

Marked similarity in the trends of outdoor relief expenditures in urban and in rural-town areas for the 48 months from January 1932 through December 1935 is displayed by the curves in figure 13. These curves, plotted from index numbers, are contrasted with a curve representing outdoor relief disbursements in urban and rural United States combined. In January 1932 the rural-town index was 18.3, the urban index 34.5, and the combined index 30.6. After the Federal Emergency Relief Administration was established, expenditures in rural areas increased at a somewhat more rapid rate than expenditures in urban areas. In January 1934 the rural-town index was 50.6 and the urban index 43.6. Emergency expenditures for drought relief during the fall and winter of 1934–1935 explain in part the rise in the rural index in that period. In January 1935 the rural index registered 139.2 as contrasted with 122.7 for the urban index. The effects of the Civil Works program and the Works Program in reducing expenditures for outdoor relief are reflected in each of the curves.

Estimated annual expenditures for outdoor relief in urban and in rural-town United States in the 4 years from 1932 through 1935 indicate that expenditures in rural-town areas have become a larger fraction of national relief expenditures, increasing from approximately

Table 20.—Estimated Expenditures for Outdoor Relief in Rural [1] and in Urban [2] United States, by Type of Assistance, 1932–1935

Type of assistance	1932		1933		1934		1935	
	Rural	Urban	Rural	Urban	Rural	Urban	Rural	Urban
				Amount in thousands				
Total outdoor relief	$85,843	$445,985	$198,005	$647,424	$344,549	$965,365	$397,169	$1,217,037
				Percent distribution				
Total outdoor relief	100.0	100.0	100.0	100.0	100.0	100.0	100.0	100.0
Public relief	97.4	81.4	98.7	93.8	99.6	97.8	99.6	98.6
General and veteran	82.6	67.8	91.0	85.1	94.5	91.5	91.1	91.8
Aid to special classes	14.8	13.6	7.7	8.7	5.1	6.3	7.9	6.8
Aid to the aged	3.5	5.2	3.2	3.1	2.5	2.4	5.5	3.5
Aid to the blind	2.1	0.8	1.0	0.6	0.7	0.5	0.6	0.5
Aid to dependent children	9.2	7.6	3.5	5.0	1.9	3.4	1.8	2.8
Resettlement emergency grants	—	—	—	—	—	—	0.6	—
Private relief	2.6	18.6	1.3	6.2	0.4	2.2	0.4	1.4

[1] Represents counties containing no city of 25,000 or over, and Massachusetts and Connecticut townships of less than 5,000.
[2] Represents counties containing cities of 25,000 or over, and Massachusetts and Connecticut townships of 5,000 and over.
Source: Unpublished data from Division of Social Research, Works Progress Administration. Estimates based on data from Rural-Town Relief Series and Urban Relief Series.

one-sixth of the total annual expenditures in 1932 to nearly one-fourth in 1935. Differences in the relative importance of the component types of relief in urban and in rural-town areas and distinct shifts in importance over the 4-year period are apparent from the percentage distribution of annual expenditures in table 20. Noteworthy is the decrease in the percentage of private relief in urban areas and the decline in the percentage of assistance to the aged, the blind, and dependent children in both urban and rural-town areas. Both of these changes can be attributed in large part to the tremendous expansion in general public (emergency) relief over this period. As has already been indicated, total assistance to the aged, to the blind, and to dependent children has increased both in absolute and relative importance since December 1935.

COMPARISON OF TRENDS OF PUBLIC OUTDOOR RELIEF IN ALL SELECTED AREAS

In the previous sections analysis has been made of data on relief expenditures of public and private agencies in selected areas and groups of areas. These data cover different spans of time within the period 1910 through 1935. In order that the separate trends may be compared to show whether they reveal similar or unlike tendencies, annual expenditures of public agencies in the different areas or groups of areas are plotted in figure 14. Although some information on expenditures of private agencies has been included in the earlier analysis, it is excluded here in order to obtain the maximum uniformity. The curves are plotted on a ratio or semilogarithmic background and consequently are strictly comparable for trend.[72]

Examination of the diagram reveals general consistency in the several curves—an upward movement in public relief expenditures over the entire period from 1910 through 1935, with a very pronounced acceleration of the rate of change in 1930 and in subsequent years. There is too little evidence for the early depression of 1914–1915 to support conclusions concerning relief expenditures in this period of business recession. It should be noted, however, that all the curves which incorporate data for the 1921–1922 depression show a decided bulge for those years, followed immediately or shortly thereafter by a continued upward movement. It is apparent that relief expenditures in the selected areas did not recede to their old levels with the return of prosperity.

In view of the fact that the curves in figure 14 represent singly or collectively very substantial portions of the United States, considerable significance can be attached to the agreement in the trends which they display. Together they offer convincing evidence of an underlying upward trend in outdoor relief expenditures during the last

---

[72] For a summary presentation of the data from which the curves were plotted, see appendix table 7.

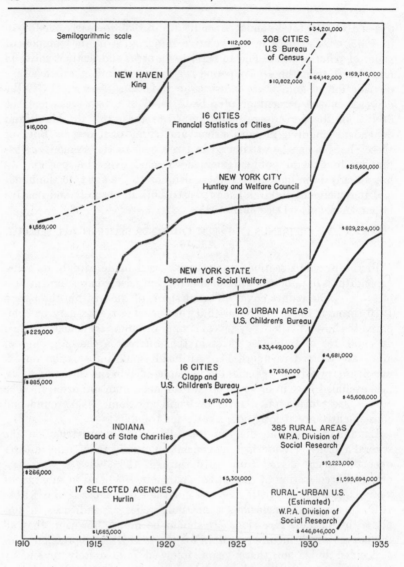

FIG. 14 – TRENDS OF EXPENDITURES FOR PUBLIC OUTDOOR
RELIEF IN SELECTED AREAS
1910-1935

Note: Broken lines indicate data not available or
not available in comparable form for these years.

Source: Compiled from sources indicated in chart.

AF–1449, W.P.A.

quarter of a century. New forms of public assistance have contributed to the increase in annual expenditures and to gradual shifts in the incidence of the relief burden from private to public resources and from local to State and Federal units of government. The assumption by the Federal Government of a part of the responsibility for caring for the needy unemployed has accelerated the upward trend in relief expenditures during recent years and has induced further shifts in the relative importance of different types of assistance.

Two important developments in relief trends are not apparent from the chart. One is the decline in the relative importance of private relief to an insignificant portion of total outdoor relief. The other is the increasing emphasis on work relief and work projects as a means of providing aid to the needy unemployed. Federal work programs have, in some instances, departed from traditional relief concepts in determining eligibility and earnings of employees and have extended assistance at a higher level of adequacy than was provided by existing relief agencies. Wage payments under these programs have been excluded from the relief series presented in Part I, so that these series understate for 1933, 1934, and 1935 the total burden of noninstitutional assistance.

Part II

Public Outdoor Relief and Wage Assistance, 1933-1935

Part II

PUBLIC OUTDOOR RELIEF AND
WAGE ASSISTANCE, 1933-1935

PART II of this report attempts to measure the national burden of public assistance, exclusive of institutional care, during the last 3 years of the quarter century ending December 31, 1935. The relief series presented in Part I have related only to selected areas and have excluded wage assistance extended through the various work programs initiated by the Federal Government during 1933 and 1935. To that extent, therefore, the series in Part I fall short of giving a complete measure of the trend and volume of public assistance in the areas and periods covered.

MEASUREMENT OF THE COMBINED RELIEF AND WAGE ASSISTANCE BURDEN

Traditional concepts of relief have assumed: (1) that relief should be given at a subsistence level; (2) that it should be given only to persons found through a means test to be in need; and (3) that it should be continued only so long as need continues. The employment programs operated by the Civil Works Administration, the Civilian Conservation Corps,[1] the Works Progress Administration, and other agencies participating in the Works Program have embodied some but not all of these concepts. Accordingly, wage payments made by these agencies were not considered relief, in the strict sense of the term, and were not incorporated in relief series currently compiled during these years.

Although these work programs have not conformed to a strict relief pattern in respect to eligibility and earnings, the wages extended have been largely a substitute for relief. Thus, these wage payments constitute a new form of public assistance that must be considered

---

[1] The more familiar designation of Civilian Conservation Corps is used to refer to the Emergency Conservation Work program, which includes, in addition to CCC, conservation work on Indian reservations and in the territories.

in conjunction with the more traditional forms of outdoor relief if we are to have a comprehensive measure of the public burden of caring for needy and distressed persons during this period. Only by constructing such a comprehensive measure does it become possible to interpret and to evaluate correctly the changes that have taken place in the trend and volume of the component parts of the public assistance structure.

The task of Part II, therefore, is to develop an integrated outdoor relief and wage assistance series for the total United States by splicing together the data on three major types of public assistance extended to families and individuals during 1933, 1934, and 1935—i. e., emergency relief,[2] categorical relief, and wage assistance.

Comprehensive data on the emergency relief and wage assistance programs are available for these 3 years largely because the Federal Government participated actively in the administration and financing of these forms of aid. The Federal Emergency Relief Administration was not established until May 1933 but its collection of emergency relief data was extended back to the beginning of that year.[3] The Federal agencies conducting wage assistance programs have also maintained monthly statistical records of their operations and expenditures. However, the Federal Government did not participate during these years in the administration or financing of categorical relief, and there was no provision for Federal collection of monthly data on categorical relief.[4] To complete the total public relief and wage assistance structure it has been necessary to estimate the volume of statutory relief extended monthly to the aged, to the blind, and to dependent children during this period.[5] For reasons which will be presented in the section immediately following, the consolidated series based on expenditures has not been supplemented with a consolidated case series.

Descriptions of the data included under each of the major classes of aid are given in succeeding sections of the report. Individual programs are discussed only as far as necessary to explain their inclusion in the series and their relation to the total public assistance structure, which is presented in the concluding sections of Part II.

---

[2] The term "emergency relief" is practically analogous to the term "general relief" as used in Part I of this report, but it includes in addition to direct and work relief a small amount of specialized relief, which will be described subsequently.

[3] These early data are partially estimated. Summary reports on monthly expenditures were obtained directly from the States; estimates on case loads were prepared from State records.

[4] Some annual data on categorical relief were collected prior to 1936 by the Bureau of Labor Statistics and by the Children's Bureau of the U. S. Department of Labor. See appendix D. Since January 1936 data on categorical relief have been collected by the Social Security Board for all States qualifying for Federal grants-in-aid and for some other States reporting voluntarily.

[5] See appendix D for methodological note on estimates.

A group of charts analyzing the trend and volume of emergency relief under the general relief program of the FERA is presented at the end of the report to illustrate the necessity for interpreting changes in this one class of assistance in the light of changes occurring concurrently in other classes. The charts serve the further important purpose of demonstrating the extreme variations in State relief patterns which underlie the consolidated series for the total United States.

Individual judgments will differ as to the desirability or appropriateness of incorporating in an integrated series all of the items that have been included here. The attempt has been made to include expenditures of all programs which had any definite relief attributes, but in view of the controversial nature of various items the composition of the series has been described in detail, and attention has been directed to the inclusion or exclusion of specific expenditures concerning which there is likely to be difference of opinion. Opportunity is thereby offered for the reader to appraise the validity of the series and to make such adjustment as he wishes within the limitations of the primary data. Other types of integrated series could be developed which would differ both in content and in major classifications of data. It might be desirable in certain instances to segregate the data according to a direct relief-work classification or to develop a series which would exclude payments to persons not certified as in need.

The series developed here is not strictly a relief series, since it includes payments to employees whose need had not been established by application of the means test. Payments to uncertified employees on the Works Program and to employees of the Civil Works Administration and Civilian Conservation Corps who were not drawn from relief rolls have been included in order to present a complete picture of persons benefiting from the wage assistance programs. The nonrelief nonadministrative persons on the FERA Emergency Work Program were included for a similar reason. The wage assistance programs departed in various ways from previous concepts of relief as regards eligibility and level of assistance, so that it is difficult to apply any uniform criteria to determine the extent of need of persons benefiting from them.

Even if it had seemed desirable for purposes of this report to exclude payments to cases not certified or without prior relief status, it was not feasible for the entire 3-year period or for all of the programs that have been included in the series to segregate wage payments on that basis. Records of the Civil Works Administration did not distinguish between employees with previous relief status and employees drawn from the ranks of the general unemployed. Prior to July 1935 the Civilian Conservation Corps did not report enrollees according to relief status.

COMPARABILITY OF CASE-LOAD DATA

A consolidated series representing the number of cases receiving emergency relief, wage assistance, and categorical relief each month during 1933, 1934, and 1935 would afford a far more realistic measure of the extent of need and the magnitude of the public assistance burden than is afforded by the expenditure data, which are much affected by changes in the value of the dollar and by differences in standards of care.[6] Unfortunately, it is not possible to construct a composite case-load series for the period from 1933 through 1935 by direct addition of reported case figures. Comprehensive data on the number of cases receiving emergency relief were collected monthly over this period and records were also maintained of the number of persons employed on wage assistance programs. However, no monthly data are available on the number of cases receiving old-age relief, blind relief, or aid to dependent children during these years, and it is difficult to estimate national case loads for these categories of relief.

Even for the emergency relief and wage assistance programs the data on case loads cannot be added together because of lack of homogeneity in the case units and because of extensive duplication in case counts. This duplication resulted when cases received assistance from two or more programs, either concurrently or successively during a month.[7]

The number of cases given emergency relief and the number of persons receiving wage assistance under the several work programs during 1933, 1934, and 1935 are recorded by months in table 21, but the data there presented cannot be totaled to show a combined case-load trend. The term "case" as used in this table has a variety of meanings. Even among the several programs comprising the broad emergency relief program it has two distinct connotations. The case unit under the general relief, rural rehabilitation, and transient programs represents an individual, family, or other group of persons treated as an entity by the relief agency, and hence is highly variable in size and composition. Under the emergency education and college student aid programs the case represents the individual employee. The employee is also the case unit for the Civilian Conservation Corps, the Civil Works, and the Works Program agencies.

---

[6] See p. 59 for further discussion of the deficiencies of the expenditure series.

[7] An estimated monthly series representing the net total number of persons aided by emergency relief and work programs during the period 1933 through 1936 has recently been developed by the Division of Research, Statistics, and Records, Works Progress Administration. See, Ross, Emerson and Whiting, T. E., "Changes in the Number of Relief Recipients, 1933–1936," *FERA Monthly Report for June 1936*, Division of Research, Statistics, and Finance, Federal Emergency Relief Administration, 1936, pp. 1–21.

In addition to differences in the composition of the case unit, the case data for the separate programs cover different time intervals. In some instances the figures include all cases given assistance at any time during the month. In other instances they represent the number being aided at some particular period, such as the last week of the month or the peak week in the month. Because of the constant turnover in case loads, figures presented on either of these last two bases constitute an understatement of the total number aided during the month.

The fact that the case units for the different programs are not uniform does not alone preclude the addition of the case-load data in table 21. An even more serious obstacle is the continuous interplay between the emergency relief agencies and the wage assistance agencies, resulting in extensive duplication in monthly case counts. This duplication is not limited to persons and families receiving assistance from two or more agencies simultaneously, but occurs whenever cases are transferred from one program or type of assistance to another during the course of a month. Accordingly, duplication in case counts is greatest during the periods of transition from one major program to another. No comprehensive data are available to measure the duplication in monthly case counts arising either through such transfers or through concurrent assistance extended by different agencies,[8] but some idea of the sources and extent of such duplication can be gained by a brief examination of the administrative relationships which existed between the various relief and wage assistance programs.

From the time the Civilian Conservation Corps was established in April 1933 there has been some duplication between the case counts of that program and those of the emergency relief agencies. The majority of the young men enrolled in the Civilian Conservation Corps were recruited from families on emergency relief rolls. These enrollees were, for the most part, required to contribute a substantial share of their earnings to their families. This contribution was sufficient in some instances to remove the family from the emergency relief rolls, but in other instances the family remained on relief during

---

[8] See footnote 7, p. 54. The Administrator of the Works Progress Administration estimated the amount of duplication between cases on the rolls of the emergency relief agencies and on the rolls of the wage assistance agencies as 337,000 in January 1934; as 84,000 in January 1935; and as 1,020,000 in January 1936. A still greater volume of duplication unquestionably occurred in months other than those cited, when the Civil Works program was in process of organization or liquidation and when the Works Program was in the organization stage. See statements of Harry L. Hopkins, First Deficiency Appropriation Bill for 1936, *Extract from Hearing Before the Subcommittee of House Committee on Appropriations in Charge of Deficiency Appropriations*, 74th Cong., 2d sess., 1936, pp. 206–208.

Table 21.—Cases [1] Receiving Emergency Relief and Wage Assistance, Continental United States, January 1933–December 1935 [2]

Cases in thousands [1]

Year and month	Emergency relief										Wage assistance				
	Total emergency relief, exclusive of nonrelief employees and transients	General relief program, FERA, and other emergency relief agencies				Special programs, FERA				Resettlement Administration (emergency grants)	Civil Works Administration	Civil Works Service	Civilian Conservation Corps [5]	Works Progress Administration	Other Works Program agencies [6]
		Total general relief, exclusive of nonrelief employees	Direct relief only	Work relief	Nonrelief employees not on administrative projects [3]	Emergency education	Rural rehabilitation	College student aid	Transient [4]						
1933															
January	4,290 [7]	4,290 [7]	2,720 [7]	1,570 [7]	(8)	—	—	—	(9)	—	—	—	—	—	—
February	4,610 [7]	4,610 [7]	2,880 [7]	1,730 [7]	(8)	—	—	—	(9)	—	—	—	—	—	—
March	5,080 [7]	5,080 [7]	3,110 [7]	1,970 [7]	(8)	—	—	—	(9)	—	—	—	—	—	—
April	4,914 [7]	4,914 [7]	2,965 [7]	1,949 [7]	(8)	—	—	—	(9)	—	—	—	40	—	—
May	4,723 [7]	4,723 [7]	2,821 [7]	1,902 [7]	(8)	—	—	—	(9)	—	—	—	190	—	—
June	4,191 [7]	4,191 [7]	2,547 [7]	1,645 [7]	(8)	—	—	—	(9)	—	—	—	270	—	—
July	3,908	3,908	2,229	1,679	(8)	—	—	—	(9)	—	—	—	305	—	—
August	3,761	3,761	2,042	1,718	(8)	—	—	—	(9)	—	—	—	291	—	—
September	3,405	3,405	1,965	1,439	(8)	—	—	—	(9)	—	—	—	223	—	—
October	3,445	3,445	1,981	1,464	(8)	(9)	—	—	(9)	—	—	37	276	—	—
November	3,829	3,827	2,275	1,553	(8)	2	—	—	(9)	—	1,475	141	336	—	—
December	3,078	3,068	2,901	167	(8)	10	(9)	(9)	(9)	—	3,438	—	313	—	—
1934															
January	2,954	2,928	2,835	93	(8)	25	—	1	(9)	—	3,879	212	327	—	—
February	3,153	3,088	2,993	95	(8)	33	—	31	104	—	3,216	126 [10]	317	—	—
March	3,697	3,603	3,443	160	(8)	33	—	60	135	—	1,886	—	243	—	—
April	4,445	4,355	3,267	1,088	97	24	(9)	66	167	—	38	—	309	—	—
May	4,435	4,337	2,976	1,362	67	17	18	62	184	—	1	—	330	—	—
June	4,331	4,261	2,756	1,505	62	8	27	34	204	—	—	—	275	—	—
July	4,395	4,356	2,630	1,725	63	9	31	(11)	244	—	—	—	383	—	—
August	4,620	4,576	2,652	1,924	64	9	34	(11)	273	—	—	—	379	—	—
September	4,742	4,620	2,668	1,952	63	13	40	69	261	—	—	—	330	—	—
October	4,814	4,649	2,648	2,000	68	23	46	96	268	—	—	—	386	—	—
November	5,004	4,821	2,656	2,165	76	31	52	100	268	—	—	—	381	—	—
December	5,281	5,078	2,774	2,303	78	34	69	100	243	—	—	—	344	—	—

1935

Month														
January	5,490	5,276	2,830	2,446	72	40	72	102	246	—	—	392	—	—
February	5,473	5,240	2,806	2,435	67	42	87	103	240	—	—	367	—	—
March	5,494	5,172	2,802	2,370	54	44	173	105	281	—	—	288	—	—
April	5,371	5,013	2,737	2,276	57	44	210	104	288	—	—	362	—	—
May	5,188	4,842	2,645	2,197	58	41	205	100	281	—	—	376	—	6
June	4,822	4,534	2,512	2,021	63	32	204	52	269	—	—	418	—	13
July	4,397	4,369	2,440	1,929	62	28	(12)	(11)	263	—	—	470	(9)	59
August	4,250	4,218	2,807	1,411	52	32	(12)	(11)	249	—	—	380	157	110
September	3,933	3,908	3,019	889	29	25	(12)	(13)	170	—	—	524	[14] 411	162
October	3,741	3,722	3,077	645	19	19	(12)	(13)	140	—	—	541	[14] 929	214
November	3,485	3,462	3,116	346	13	17	(12)	(13)	110	6	—	534	[14] 2,081	214
December	2,746	2,608	2,549	59	7	8	(13)	(13)	83	130	—	497	[14] 3,014	252

[1] The term "case" as used here refers to individuals employed on work programs as well as family and nonfamily cases receiving relief on a budget deficiency basis. Administrative employees are excluded. All figures are rounded independently to the nearest thousand so that totals may not equal the exact sum of the parts.

[2] Monthly data on case loads for the several programs refer to different periods of time, as follows: Emergency relief, exclusive of payments to nonrelief employees not on administrative projects, all cases receiving relief during the month; nonrelief employees not on administrative projects, number employed during peak week of month; transients, estimated number receiving relief during the month; Civil Works Administration and Civil Works Service, number employed during last week of month; Civilian Conservation Corps, peak number of persons at work during month; Works Progress Administration and other Works Program agencies, number employed at any time during month. The data for rural rehabilitation include only cases receiving advances during the month indicated.

[3] Includes nonrelief persons working on the ERA Work Program whose services are charged to specific work projects or tool and sundry equipment projects.

[4] Estimates made by Division of Social Research, WPA, of family and unattached cases receiving relief during the month under Federal transient program. Estimates based on midmonthly census and total registration figures.

[5] Includes Indians employed by ECW in conservation work on Indian reservations. Excludes reserve officers.

[6] See appendix C for complete list of Federal Government units participating in the Works Program as of December 31, 1935.

[7] Estimated or partially estimated.

[8] Not available.

[9] Fewer than 500 cases.

[10] The Civil Works Service projects, for clerical and professional persons, were essentially a part of the CWA program, although financed from emergency relief funds. They were absorbed by CWA during February 1934. The peak of CWA employment, exclusive of CWS, was 3,983,000 during the week ending January 18, 1934. Liquidation of the program began shortly thereafter. Employment during the week ending March 15 was 2,368,000.

[11] Not in operation in summer months.

[12] Transferred to Resettlement Administration. That agency continued to make loans for rehabilitation purposes, which were gradually placed on a stricter financial basis. Included in WPA beginning September 1, 1935.

[13] Transferred to National Youth Administration. Cases receiving these loans have been omitted from the data, as have a small number of cases that received advances from State rural rehabilitation corporations after July 1, 1935.

[14] Cases receiving aid under National Youth Administration included as follows: September, 35,000; October, 184,000; November, 234,000; December, 282,000.

Source: Data for emergency relief were obtained from the Division of Research, Statistics, and Records of the Works Progress Administration and from Resettlement Administration; those for wage assistance from the Division of Research, Statistics, and Records of the Works Progress Administration, the National Youth Administration, the Bureau of Labor Statistics, and the Office of Emergency Conservation Work.

part or all of the enrollee's period of enlistment.[9] Even if the family was dropped from the emergency relief rolls, there was some overlap in case counts for the month of enrollment.

Very extensive duplication existed between cases on emergency relief rolls and cases on the rolls of the Civil Works Administration. The latter agency, which operated for about 4½ months, was expected to draw one-half of its maximum number of employees from relief rolls before accepting applications from the general unemployed group. Several weeks of the brief span of operation of this program were required to bring employment to its peak of 4,192,000 persons,[10] and several additional weeks were required for liquidation of the program and the reabsorption into the emergency relief program of employees able to meet the needs test.

Again, with the development of the Works Program in the second half of 1935, there was a large-scale movement of cases from the emergency relief rolls to the rolls of the various Works Program agencies. This movement was likewise accompanied by a large amount of duplicate recording of cases. Movement was principally to the rolls of the Works Progress Administration, which absorbed employable persons from the general relief program and also from the emergency education and transient programs. The fact that emergency relief administrations were urged to furnish relief allowances to all relief cases transferred to the Works Progress Administration for a period sufficient to maintain the cases until the receipt of the first pay check contributed further to duplication in case counts during the period of transfer.

Not only was there duplication between the emergency relief agencies on the one hand and the wage assistance agencies on the other, but there was also some duplication between the wage assistance agencies themselves. This duplication existed particularly between the Civilian Conservation Corps and the Works Progress Administration and between the Works Progress Administration and the National Youth Administration. Duplication also arose from cases receiving some form of categorical relief in addition to emergency relief or wage assistance.

It is evident from the above discussion that reported case data for the period from 1933 through 1935, although far more comprehensive and adequate than any previously compiled, do not provide complete information for an integrated monthly series measuring with precision

---

[9] Unpublished data from a special survey made by the Division of Research, Statistics, and Finance of the Federal Emergency Relief Administration in the winter of 1934–35 indicate that approximately 37 percent of the families represented by former CCC enrollees were removed from the relief rolls as a result of the CCC enrollment.

[10] For the week ending January 18, 1934. This figure is exclusive of persons employed on administrative projects.

the unduplicated number of cases benefiting from public relief and assistance programs. It should be equally apparent that changes occurring in the emergency relief load during this period cannot be properly interpreted except in the light of changes that occurred in the case loads for other forms of aid.

Until the case unit is standardized with respect to the period covered and workable techniques are developed for eliminating duplication in case counts as between agencies,[11] it will be difficult, without extensive estimating, to construct an integrated monthly series which will reflect the interplay between the three forms of public assistance. Some administrative adjustment and integration of the various assistance programs is a necessary step in the achievement of more adequate case data. In the meantime, the expenditure data afford a more satisfactory measure of the volume and trend of the total public assistance burden.

LIMITATIONS OF EXPENDITURE SERIES

As indicated earlier, an expenditure series also has distinct limitations. Monthly expenditures for the various programs are, of course, expressed in dollar units and can be combined without duplication to show the total monthly expenditures for relief and wage assistance in a given area. These monthly data provide an accurate measure of the trend and volume of relief costs, but are not entirely satisfactory as a measure of relief need because they reflect differences in the cost of living and in the level of care provided. Hence there is no simple and direct relationship between changes in expenditures and changes in case loads.

The effect of cost of living changes on the trend of relief expenditures has been illustrated in Part I.[12] A general rise in relief standards and the introduction of new types of relief providing more liberal relief allowances were also noted as having contributed to the upward trend in outdoor relief expenditures. Since the initiation of Federal emergency relief and employment programs, these variations in standards of care have been more pronounced, and their effect on relief trends has been accentuated by rapid administrative shifts from one type of assistance program to another. Thus, the transfer of cases from the subsistence benefits of the early FERA program to the regular wage payments of the Civil Works Administration, the transfer of cases back to the emergency relief rolls, and the subsequent assignment of cases to the security wage payments of the Works Program have produced fluctuations in the combined expenditure trend which do not coincide with fluctuations in the combined case loads of these agencies.

---

[11] Progress had been made by individual States in eliminating duplication in case data, but techniques for this purpose have not yet been applied nationally.

[12] See pp. 13, 16, and 18 ff.

The differences in eligibility requirements and in levels of payments under the work programs explain, in large part, the omission of wage assistance data from current relief series. Nevertheless, these differences do not seem to justify the exclusion of this type of assistance from an integrated expenditure series intended to reflect changes in the total burden of public assistance outside of institutions.[13] It is, of course, extremely important to consider the effects of the higher standards of assistance in interpreting the combined trend of expenditures for relief and wage assistance and to differentiate clearly between changes in expenditures and changes in case loads.

COMPONENT PARTS OF THE PUBLIC ASSISTANCE BURDEN

The combined volume of public emergency relief, wage assistance, and categorical relief extended to families and individuals in the United States in the 3 years 1933, 1934, and 1935 is estimated as approximately $5,375,000,000. This figure does not include expenses for administrative purposes, expenses for materials, supplies, and equipment, or certain other expenses incident to the operation of the relief and wage assistance programs.[14] The grand total of all expenditures of agencies administering relief and wage assistance in 1933, 1934, and 1935 would be substantially higher. The percentage distribution of the $5,375,000,000 extended to cases, shown in figure 15, indicates that more than 65 percent of the total was for emergency relief, 30 percent for wage assistance, and less than 5 percent for categorical relief.

Obligations incurred [15] for emergency relief, including direct relief, work relief, and some specialized aid administered by the Federal Emergency Relief Administration and State and local emergency relief agencies, amounted to approximately $3,513,000,000. Wage assistance, or earnings of employees of the Civilian Conservation Corps, the Civil Works Administration and Civil Works Service, the Works Progress Administration, and other Works Program agencies, amounted to $1,605,000,000. Expenditures for three categories of dependents, the aged, the blind, and dependent children, are estimated at roughly

---

[13] It should be noted that the relief series themselves include data from various types of private and public relief agencies, extending care at widely different levels of adequacy.

[14] With the exception of small amounts of nonrelief expenditures for some of the special programs of the FERA. In the case of these special programs data representing total obligations incurred have been used, since administrative and other costs incident to their operation cannot be segregated over the entire period.

[15] Monthly data for emergency relief represent amounts "obligated" for relief during the period; those for wage assistance and categorical relief represent amounts "expended." This distinction is maintained in the discussion of the component parts, but in the consolidated tables and charts the term "expenditures" has been used to cover both types of financial transactions. Over a period of time "expenditures" tend to approximate "obligations incurred."

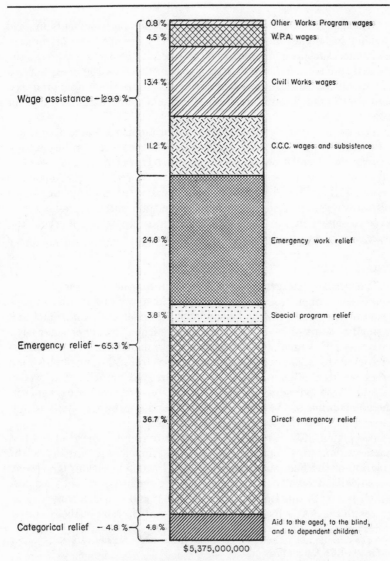

Wage assistance —29.9 %

0.8 %   Other Works Program wages
4.5 %   W.P.A. wages
13.4 %   Civil Works wages
11.2 %   C.C.C. wages and subsistence

Emergency relief —65.3 %

24.8 %   Emergency work relief
3.8 %   Special program relief
36.7 %   Direct emergency relief

Categorical relief — 4.8 %   4.8 %   Aid to the aged, to the blind, and to dependent children

$5,375,000,000

FIG. 15 —PERCENT DISTRIBUTION OF TOTAL EXPENDITURES *
FOR PUBLIC RELIEF AND WAGE ASSISTANCE
IN THE UNITED STATES
1933-1935

*Represents amounts extended to families and individuals.
Excludes administrative and other costs incident to the
operation of the relief and wage assistance programs.

Source: Division of Research, Statistics, and Records,
Works Progress Administration. Estimates of categorical
relief based on miscellaneous sources listed in appendix D.

AF-1463, W.P.A.

$257,000,000. These sums represent substantially payments in cash or kind to families and individuals.[16] They are exclusive of the cost of Federal surplus commodities distributed in the 3 years through the American Red Cross, the Federal Surplus Relief, and Federal Surplus Commodities Corporations and of the cost of commodities produced and distributed through work relief projects set up for production for use.

The technical difficulties involved in attaching a value to surplus commodities are very great, and statistical data concerning the monthly distribution have been compiled only in terms of quantities issued.[17] In some communities surplus commodities comprised an important share of the relief distributed, and omission of their value would result in a serious understatement of the total outdoor public assistance extended in the area. For the United States as a whole the omission is less important.

Emergency Relief

The term "emergency relief" came into common usage in the depression when emergency appropriations were made to finance general relief programs. It includes both direct and work relief and a small amount of relief to special groups cared for under the FERA program. Emergency relief has not, as its name might suggest, been restricted to families whose need arose from the unemployment crisis or from other hazards, such as drought or flood, but has in practice been extended in some degree to other classes of dependents, including some of the aged, the blind, and dependent children, not provided for by statutory categorical relief.

The period 1933 through 1935 extends over two phases of Federal participation in emergency relief. The first phase antedates the creation of the Federal Emergency Relief Administration; the second phase coincides with the period of active operation of that agency, which began to function on May 23, 1933, and had determined final grants to the States by December 1935 in anticipation of the complete

---

[16] The data do not include, for example, grants made for self-help cooperatives or for the FERA land program.

[17] For summary statement of quantities of goods distributed by the Red Cross, see American Red Cross, *The Distribution of Government-Owned Wheat and Cotton*, June 1, 1934, pp. 80–83. The total amount expended for Government wheat and cotton distribution in 1932 and 1933 was $73,598,452. This includes processing and transportation costs but excludes administrative expenses. For data on surplus commodities distributed monthly through the FSRC and FSCC from October 4, 1933, to December 31, 1935, see Federal Surplus Commodities Corporation, *Report of the Federal Surplus Commodities Corporation for the Calendar Year of 1935*, April 1, 1936, pp. 10–11. Expenditures during this period, chargeable to State grants for commodities, processing, and transportation, totaled $123,397,493. *Ibid.*, p. 8.

withdrawal of the Federal Government from emergency relief operations.[18]

In the first phase of Federal participation emergency relief was administered by State and local agencies not subject to Federal administrative control, but some of these agencies were financed in part by Federal funds advanced to the States and localities on a loan basis through the Emergency Relief Division of the Reconstruction Finance Corporation.[19] In the second phase emergency relief was administered primarily by State and local emergency relief administrations under the supervision of the Federal Emergency Relief Administration, which made grants-in-aid to the States and prescribed rules and regulations pertaining to eligibility, standards, and procedures. In some instances these State and local administrations represented a continuity of organizations which had operated earlier; in other instances they were entirely new administrative units. But in either case they were subject to some degree of Federal control. Where new administrative machinery was set up the old machinery was virtually displaced, even though the statutory basis for its functioning remained.

Data used in this section relating to emergency relief are those reported to the Federal Emergency Relief Administration.[20] During the period of operation of the FERA the data represent substantially but not exclusively obligations incurred for relief by State and local emergency relief administrations. Small amounts of local poor relief and veteran relief continued to be extended by agencies not reimbursed from Federal funds and thus not subject to Federal regulation. Some but not all of this local poor relief and veteran relief was reported by the States. For the United States as a whole the data presented here for emergency relief are believed to represent substantially the total volume of public outdoor relief disbursed, exclusive of categorical relief and of the value of surplus commodities.

Emergency relief was extended to needy clients on the basis of investigation, either in the form of direct relief allowances or work relief wages. Both types of benefits were adjusted in amount to the budget deficiency of the relief case, except for those cases aided by the college student aid, rural rehabilitation, and transient programs, and were distributed either in cash or kind. The data reported to FERA on

---

[18] The Federal Emergency Relief Administration was continued after December 1935, but only for purposes of liquidation.

[19] See footnote 54, p. 33.

[20] Except in November and December 1935 when emergency grants of the Resettlement Administration are also included. These emergency grants amounted to $99,000 in November and to $2,442,000 in December.

Table 22.—Expenditures[1] for Emergency Relief, Wage Assistance, and Categorical Relief, Continental United States, January 1933–December 1935

[Amount in thousands[5]]

Year and month	Total all programs	Emergency relief — Total emergency relief	General relief program, FERA, and other emergency agencies — Direct relief	Work relief[1]	Special programs, FERA — Emergency education[1]	Rural rehabilitation[1]	College student aid	Transient[1]	Resettlement Administration (emergency grants)	Wage assistance — Total wage assistance	Civil Works Administration[1]	Civil Works Service	Civilian Conservation Corps[3]	Works Progress Administration	Other Works Program agencies[4]	Categorical relief (estimated)[2] — Total categorical relief	Aid to the aged	Aid to the blind	Aid to dependent children
Total, all periods	$5,374,867	$3,512,990	$1,972,918	$1,331,045	$34,101	$57,924	$14,930	$99,529	$2,541	$1,604,997	$663,936	$24,059	$601,710	$244,379	$40,593	$256,880	$122,880	$21,640	$112,360
Year 1933																			
Total	1,093,000	743,505	481,969	256,499	415	—	[3]	4,619	—	280,304	166,147	5,840	108,317	—	—	69,190	25,840	6,600	36,750
First half	454,828	397,201	256,804	139,148	—	—	—	1,250	—	22,707	—	—	22,707	—	—	34,920	13,090	3,250	18,580
January	[2]63,996	[2]57,956	[2]39,051	[2]18,905	—	—	—	—	—	—	—	—	—	—	—	6,040	2,230	530	3,280
February	[2]69,806	[2]63,966	[2]42,453	[2]21,513	—	—	—	—	—	—	—	—	—	—	—	5,840	2,240	540	3,060
March	[2]82,671	[2]76,821	[2]50,201	[2]26,619	—	—	—	—	—	—	—	—	—	—	—	5,850	2,190	540	3,120
April	74,976	69,115	44,325	24,312	—	—	—	[2]478	—	—	—	—	—	—	—	5,760	2,160	540	3,060
May	81,423	66,958	41,348	25,169	—	—	—	[2]441	—	100	—	—	100	—	—	5,750	2,140	550	3,060
June	81,937	62,385	39,425	22,630	—	—	—	[2]331	—	8,715	—	—	8,715	—	—	5,680	2,130	550	3,000
Second half	638,172	346,304	225,166	117,352	415	—	[3]	3,369	—	257,598	166,147	5,840	85,610	—	—	34,270	12,750	3,350	18,170
July	76,650	56,595	34,675	21,581	—	—	—	339	—	14,385	—	—	14,385	—	—	5,670	2,120	550	3,000
August	75,865	57,514	33,401	23,796	—	—	—	316	—	12,662	—	—	12,662	—	—	5,690	2,110	550	3,030
September	72,751	55,081	32,788	21,966	—	—	—	328	—	11,989	—	—	11,989	—	—	5,680	2,120	560	3,000
October	81,120	60,506	35,254	24,826	4	—	—	422	—	14,925	—	—	14,925	—	—	5,690	2,120	560	3,010
November	109,783	65,830	43,377	21,715	61	—	—	677	—	38,213	21,181	627	16,405	—	—	5,740	2,140	560	3,040
December	222,003	50,779	45,671	3,468	350	—	[3]	1,287	—	165,424	144,966	5,213	15,245	—	—	5,800	2,140	570	3,090

Year 1934

Period																		
Total	2,073,325	1,236,050	656,538	507,859	13,051	8,681	7,790	42,132	760,375	527,809	18,219	214,348				76,900	32,570	7,070	37,260
First half	1,147,306	469,405	304,472	137,982	6,735	1,563	3,370	15,282	641,051	527,806	18,219	95,026				36,850	14,690	3,450	18,710
January	291,454	48,233	43,752	1,561	1,056		19	1,844	237,281	211,884		15,845					2,260	570	3,110
February	236,068	51,191	45,851	1,705	1,480		325	1,830	178,907	155,774		14,870				5,845	2,330	570	3,090
March	227,468	62,591	54,544	3,395	1,670		846	2,392	158,737	14,059	9,552	16,194				5,990	2,410	570	3,160
April	129,646	93,253	54,932	33,805	1,247		946	2,709	17,765	329	8,263	17,436				6,140	2,470	580	3,000
May	133,648	109,603	51,104	48,964	385	520	923	3,367	18,108		[6] 403	18,096				6,280	2,570	580	3,090
June	129,002	104,535		48,554		1,042	311	3,139								6,360	2,650	580	3,130
Second half	926,019	766,645	352,066	369,876	6,316	7,118	4,420	26,850	119,324	3		119,322				40,050	17,880	3,620	18,550
July	133,810	108,071	50,179	53,309	376	686	[7]	3,520	19,339			19,336				6,400	2,730	590	3,080
August	148,422	121,715	52,951	61,678	595	783	[7]	4,067	20,257			20,257				6,450	2,790	590	3,070
September	141,106	115,053	59,614	55,864	547	1,133	547	4,013	19,563	3		19,563				6,490	2,840	600	3,050
October	156,053	128,254	63,224	60,067	1,192	1,273	1,267	4,841	21,189			21,189				6,610	2,900	610	3,100
November	169,947	142,920	71,506	70,091	1,741	1,539	1,340	4,984	20,267			20,267				6,760	3,050	610	3,100
December	176,682	150,633		68,808	1,866	1,703	1,266	5,423	18,709			18,709				7,340	3,570	620	3,150

Year 1935

Period																		
Total	2,208,541	1,533,434	834,412	566,687	20,635	49,243	7,138	52,779	564,317	2,541		279,045	244,379	40,893		110,790	64,470	7,970	38,350
First half	1,102,367	938,028	427,531	409,490	13,862	49,243	7,138	30,764	112,988			112,715	244,379	273		51,350	28,530	3,870	18,950
January	194,476	166,899	77,535	77,952	2,421	1,957	1,346	5,689	19,517			19,517				8,060	4,270	630	3,160
February	180,991	153,936	72,802	68,751	2,334	3,782	1,346	4,921	18,845			18,845				8,210	4,460	640	3,110
March	184,622	159,756	75,482	66,949	2,530	8,100	1,380	5,315	16,416			16,416				8,450	4,650	640	3,160
April	186,688	159,740	71,969	66,463	2,459	12,426	1,385	5,038	18,257			18,257				8,690	4,850	650	3,190
May	185,113	157,634	67,061	69,514	2,415	12,244	1,297	5,101	18,599			18,598				8,880	5,050	650	3,180
June	170,477	140,063	62,681	59,861	1,703	10,735	384	4,699	21,354			21,082	244,379	273		9,060	5,250	660	3,150
Second half	1,106,175	595,406	406,880	157,196	6,773		[8]	22,015	451,329	2,541		166,330		40,620		59,440	35,940	4,100	19,400
July	166,096	130,924	73,375	58,798	1,502		[8]	4,893	25,841			25,132		707		9,330	5,450	670	3,210
August	168,866	121,604	71,659	43,423	1,836		[8]	4,971	29,799			29,799	2	2,600		9,550	5,660	670	3,220
September	161,471	120,811	77,215	23,753	1,211		[8]	4,187	37,712			28,709	5,312	5,398		9,740	5,870	680	3,190
October	183,284	101,693	67,598	19,879	985		[8]	3,612	50,921			29,003	[11] 16,813	8,298		10,020	6,080	680	3,250
November	196,762	80,475	67,598	9,298	848		[8]	2,633 [10] 99	71,571			28,025	[11] 34,270	10,921		10,230	6,320	690	3,220
December	229,696	59,399	53,304	2,045	391		[8]	1,718 [10] 2,442	159,228	2,541		25,661 [11] 120,872	[11] 67,110	12,694		10,570	6,560	700	3,310

[1] Excludes expenditures for administrative purposes, for purchases of materials, supplies, and equipment, and for miscellaneous purposes, with the exception of small amounts of such expenditures for the emergency education, rural rehabilitation, and transient programs. Beginning with May 1934 expenditures for work relief include earnings of nonrelief employees not on administrative projects. Data for Civil Works Administration include hire paid to owner-drivers of teams, trucks, and mechanical equipment.

[2] Estimated. See appendix D for method of estimating categorical relief.

[3] Includes subsistence. Includes also wages and subsistence for Indians employed by ECW on conservation work on Indian reservations.

[4] See appendix C for complete list of Federal Government units participating in the Works Program as of December 31, 1935.

[5] All figures rounded independently to nearest thousand so that totals may not equal the exact sum of the parts.

[6] CWS projects were transferred to CWA after February 1934.

[7] Not in operation during summer months.

[8] Transferred to Resettlement Administration. Loans made by that agency are omitted from the data as are a few advances made by State rural rehabilitation corporations after July 1, 1935. Emergency grants for subsistence begun in November 1935 are included.

[9] Transferred to National Youth Administration. Included in WPA beginning September 1, 1935.

[10] Vouchers certified for emergency grants.

[11] Includes student aid under National Youth Administration.

Source: Data for emergency relief were obtained from the Division of Research, Statistics, and Records of the Works Progress Administration, as follows: September, $221,000; October, $1,653,000; November, $2,095,000; December, $2,395,000. tration; those for wage assistance from the Division of Research, Statistics, and Records of the Works Progress Administration, the National Youth Administration, the Bureau of Labor Statistics, and the Office of Emergency Conservation Work; those for categorical relief are estimates based on miscellaneous sources described in appendix D.

obligations incurred for emergency relief represent cash payments plus the value of relief in kind.[21]

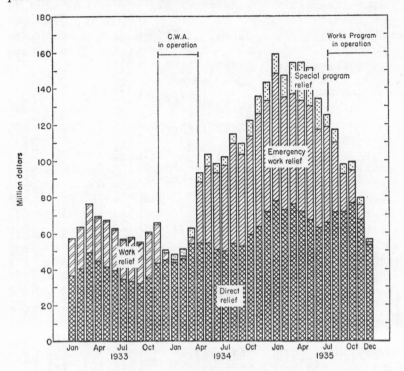

FIG. 16 – OBLIGATIONS INCURRED FOR EMERGENCY RELIEF
EXTENDED TO CASES, F.E.R.A.

January 1933 – December 1935

Source: Division of Research, Statistics, and
Records, Works Progress Administration.

AF-1447, W.P.A.

Obligations incurred for emergency relief extended to cases in the 3 years from 1933 through 1935 totaled $3,513,000,000, of which $3,307,000,000, or 94 percent, was given in the form of general direct and work relief.[22] The remaining $206,000,000 was distributed through specialized programs operated by the Federal Emergency Relief Administration to aid particular groups of dependents. These special programs were the emergency education, rural rehabilitation, college student aid, and transient programs. Amounts expended

---

[21] Relief agencies followed diverse methods in determining the cash value of relief commodities distributed during a month so that the data reported are not absolutely uniform in this respect.

[22] Emergency grants made by the Resettlement Administration are included as direct relief.

monthly for direct and work relief and for relief under each of the special programs in the 3 years are given in table 22. The volume of obligations incurred for direct and work relief and for all of the special programs combined are recorded in figure 16. This chart represents the first segment of a consolidated chart, presented later in this section,[23] which includes also data for wage assistance and categorical relief.

Direct Relief

It is evident that direct relief formed the backbone of the emergency relief program. It was administered in a continuous and growing stream over the 3-year period, with a slight seasonal movement in each of the 3 years. For 1933, 1934, and 1935 obligations incurred for direct relief aggregated $1,973,000,000. The greatest volume of direct relief was distributed in 1935. The peak in this type of relief was reached in January 1935, when obligations totaled $77,535,000. That level was substantially maintained, with only a slight slump in the summer months, until November 1935, when there was a marked decline. The high level of direct relief during the period of organization of the Works Program is probably accounted for by the shifting of cases from work to direct relief pending full development of the Works Program and by the payment of direct relief to cases transferred to the Works Program but awaiting their first pay checks. The sharp drop in direct relief in December 1935 presaged the complete withdrawal of the Federal Government from emergency relief in 1936.

Work Relief

In contrast to direct relief, work relief was administered discontinuously in two separate phases: the work relief projects prior to the Civil Works Administration and the emergency work relief program following. The early work relief projects were initiated by the States and localities before the Federal Emergency Relief Administration was established. They continued thereafter, subject to rules and regulations prescribed by the Federal Emergency Relief Administration, until the creation of the Civil Works Administration in November 1933. Work projects on a straight relief basis came to a virtual close at that time. The Emergency Work Relief Program of the FERA was inaugurated in April 1934 when the Civil Works program was terminated, and it tapered off gradually in the second half of 1935 with the development of the Works Program. As is evident from figure 16, expenditures for the early work relief projects were relatively small in comparison with those for the Emergency Work Relief Program.

[23] See p. 75.

Work relief is included as emergency relief rather than as wage assistance, because FERA clients on work relief were subject to the same regulations in respect to need as were direct relief clients, and their earnings were scaled to budget deficiency in the same manner as the direct relief benefit. Furthermore, FERA work relief expenditures have been commonly included in existing relief series, while wage assistance has been excluded.

Beginning with May 1934 the data for the Emergency Work Relief Program include work relief payments to employees without relief status who were engaged on projects of a nonadministrative character.[24] Between May 1934 and December 1935 such payments to nonrelief persons amounted to $101,324,000.

Special Program Relief

The special programs sponsored by the FERA were separately administered and were financed from earmarked grants, although some of them were not more specialized in character than various work relief projects under the general relief program, notably those for professional and technical workers. Special program relief constitutes a very small part of the total volume of assistance. It is not included in either the Urban Relief Series or the Rural and Town Relief Series, but is incorporated in this consolidated series for two reasons: one, it has a definite relief character; two, it is necessary to insure continuity between the emergency relief and wage assistance data. Most of the activities of the special programs were taken over by the Works Program agencies, and wage assistance extended for them is included in the data for that program during the latter months of the series.[25]

---

[24] There is no essential difference between such payments and payments under wage assistance programs to workers selected from the general unemployed. They are retained in the emergency relief data because they were an integral part of the FERA Work Relief Program.

[25] An exception has been made in the case of the rural rehabilitation activities which were taken over by the Resettlement Administration in July 1935. Advances made for emergency and subsistence goods under the rural rehabilitation program of the FERA are included in emergency relief, in accordance with the practice followed in FERA statistical reports. Loans made by the Resettlement Administration are excluded, although the emergency grants made by that agency are included. The differentiation in treatment of loans under the two programs is somewhat arbitrary and can be justified only by the more formal investigation procedures and financial requirements which were gradually instituted by the Resettlement Administration. Loans and commitments made by this agency during 1935 for rehabilitation purposes were to a considerable extent in completion of agreements made originally by the rural rehabilitation corporations and hence do not differ greatly from the "advances" prior to July 1935. Amounts loaned during 1935 were as follows: July, $12,645; August, $1,070,696; September, $876,946; October, $1,508,987; November, $1,965,727; December, $2,472,036. A small number of advances made by State rural rehabilitation corporations after July 1, 1935, have not been included in the data.

The transient program was authorized by the Act creating the Federal Emergency Relief Administration. Obligations incurred for transient relief were separately reported from July 1933 although earmarked grants were not made to the States until September 1933.[26] Some transient relief distributed from State and local funds prior to April 1933 is included in the data for general relief for those months.

From April 1933 through December 1935 obligations incurred specifically for transient relief totaled approximately $99,500,000. This sum includes not only relief extended in cash and kind to transients but the cost of subsistence in shelters and some other expenses incident to the operation of the Federal transient program.[27] The transient program, which was partially a work relief and partially a direct relief program, continued to operate throughout the second half of 1935, but there was marked reduction in the volume of expenditures for transients in September and in the ensuing months.[28]

The emergency education program, which was a work relief program for needy teachers, was established in October 1933 and continued operations throughout 1934 and 1935. Obligations incurred for this program, amounting to $34,000,000, include some administrative salaries and other nonrelief costs which are not separable. These items are small and do not have any appreciable effect on the series. The emergency education program was gradually absorbed by the Works Progress Administration during the latter half of 1935.

From the viewpoint of expenditures the college student aid program was the smallest of the special programs. It was in effect a work relief program designed to give limited financial assistance to needy college students. Established experimentally in Minnesota in December 1933, it was extended to other States in February 1934. Its activities were confined to the academic year. The program was transferred to the National Youth Administration as of September 1935. Total obligations incurred for college student aid prior to its transfer amounted to nearly $15,000,000. This amount is exclusive of overhead costs and represents actual amounts received by students.

The rural rehabilitation program was established in April 1934 and functioned until July 1935 when it was transferred to the Resettlement

[26] Figures for April, May, and June are estimated. It should be noted that the data on obligations incurred cover all transient relief reported to the FERA, including that given by local emergency relief administrations. These data do not match the estimated case data shown in table 22, which represent cases cared for in transient centers and camps under the Federal transient program.

[27] It is not possible to segregate administrative cost and cost of plants and equipment for the entire period. For purposes of consistency these costs have been retained in the data throughout. Total obligations incurred from July 1934 through June 1935 were $63,791,000, of which $6,247,000, or approximately 10 percent, was for materials, plants, and equipment.

[28] Intake to transient bureaus was formally closed September 20, 1935, and liquidation of case loads proceeded rapidly after that time.

Administration. During this period obligations incurred for rehabilitation and subsistence goods advanced to clients and for other costs incident to the development of the program amounted to $58,000,000. Rehabilitation and subsistence goods, for most of which notes were executed by clients, do not perhaps represent relief in the strictest sense of the term but are included with relief expenditures in view of the fact that the assistance was given in lieu of emergency relief and that opportunity was provided for working off a portion of the loans by employment on work relief projects.[29] Most of the loans were still outstanding as of the end of the year 1936. The rural rehabilitation program was carried on in 45 States, but more than 75 percent of the obligations for subsistence and rehabilitation goods were incurred in 13 States. Hence, while expenditures for the program are relatively unimportant in the national public assistance burden, they constitute an important part of the relief structure in some areas.

Wage Assistance

The term "wage assistance" has been used arbitrarily in this report to connote earnings from public work programs embodying some but not all of the traditional concepts of relief.[30] A number of Federal agencies created during the years 1933 and 1935 sponsored employment programs of a modified relief nature intended to assist needy workers, either by obviating the necessity for emergency relief or by substituting useful employment for the relief allowance. These agencies include the Civilian Conservation Corps, the Civil Works Administration, the Civil Works Service, the Works Progress Administration, and other emergency units created in connection with the broad Works Program authorized by Congress in April 1935.[31]

The public works program authorized by Title II of the National Industrial Recovery Act in June 1933 is not regarded as a wage assistance program but as an extension of normal public works. Projects were let by contracts to private employers, wages were at prevailing rates, hours of work were normal, and employees were hired in the open labor market. Accordingly, wages on these projects, including those sponsored by the Federal Emergency Administration of Public Works (PWA), are not included as wage assistance. Beginning in July 1935 many of the projects sponsored by PWA were financed from funds appropriated for the Works Program and hence were subject to the requirements that preference in employment be given to relief clients and that wages and hours be regulated to a security wage.

[29] See footnote 25, p. 68.

[30] See p. 51.

[31] The National Youth Administration, the Resettlement Administration, and the Rural Electrification Administration were other emergency units created in connection with the Works Program. A complete list of participating units will be found in appendix C.

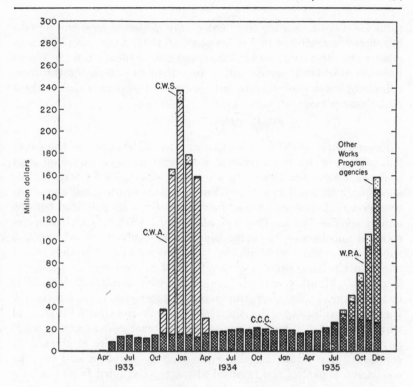

FIG. 17 – EXPENDITURES FOR WAGE ASSISTANCE
IN THE UNITED STATES
April 1933 – December 1935

Source   Division of Research, Statistics, and
Records, Works Progress Administration   A F – 1499, W.P. A.

Wages paid on these PWA projects are therefore included in the wage assistance data.

The wage assistance programs operated over widely different spans of time and varied greatly in magnitude.   They were likewise diverse in their methods of selecting employees and in determining earnings. Nevertheless, each program had a definite relief aspect and affected significantly the course of public expenditures for relief over the 3-year period.

The combined amount of wage assistance extended under the programs during the 3-year period was approximately $1,605,000,000. Monthly expenditures for earnings of workers employed by the separate agencies are shown in table 22.   The sequence of the programs and the relative volume of assistance distributed by them are shown graphically in figure 17.   It is apparent from the chart that expenditures for wage assistance were not evenly dispersed over the 3 years but were concentrated in the first half of 1934, when the CWA program was in operation, and in the second half of 1935, when the Works Program was being developed. More than two-thirds of the total volume of wage assistance for all periods was dispensed during these 2 half-year periods.

Civilian Conservation Corps

Expenditures of the Civilian Conservation Corps, first of the modified relief agencies to be created, were more evenly distributed than those of other wage assistance programs. Payment for wage assistance began in April 1933 when the CCC was created and continued uninterrupted through 1935 and subsequently. Its activities became a part of the Works Program after April 1935.[32] CCC enrollees received subsistence in camps plus the monthly wage, of which a substantial share was allotted to dependents. Through these allotments a large amount of family relief was released in the home localities. Monthly expenditures varied with enrollment levels but increased gradually over the period. Aggregate expenditures for wages and subsistence by the close of 1935 were $601,710,000, of which $456,798,000 was for wages. Subsistence cost as well as wage payments are included in the data, since subsistence is given as a supplementary return for the work done by enrollees and may be considered a part of the established wage. Excluded from the data are all administrative costs, including amounts paid to reserve officers in charge of camps.

Civil Works Administration

The Civil Works Administration operated actively for a period of about 4½ months. It was launched in November 1933 to speed the employment of needy workers and assist in the restoration of purchasing power as a basis for recovery. An employment goal of 4,000,000 was set for December 15, 1933. Two million of this number were to be taken from the relief loads prior to December 1, after which date another two million were to be taken from the general ranks of the unemployed without the application of any means test.[33]

---

[32] As of July 1, 1936, Emergency Conservation Work was removed from the Works Program and has since operated with funds provided by specific appropriations, the first of which was contained in the First Deficiency Appropriation Act, Fiscal Year 1937. See Division of Research, Statistics, and Records, Works Progress Administration, *Report on Progress of the Works Program*, October 15, 1936, pp. 49, 55.

[33] Weekly reports on CWA employment and expenditures did not distinguish between persons taken from relief rolls and persons not from relief rolls, so that it is not possible, even if it were deemed desirable, to separate the amounts dispensed to the two groups. Informal estimates indicate that considerably more than half of the total workers had relief status prior to their transfer to CWA.

Employment on CWA projects was at prevailing wage rates for normal hours. Thus, wages under the CWA program represent a distinctly higher standard of assistance than was accorded under the CCC and other wage assistance programs. The Civil Works Service was a part of the Civil Works program. It was formed to sponsor work projects for clerical and professional workers, who could not be employed on the construction projects of the regular CWA program. These projects were financed from FERA funds until February 1934, when they were absorbed into the regular CWA program.

The total amount expended for wage assistance under the short-lived CWA and CWS programs was approximately $718,000,000,[34] equal to almost 45 percent of all expenditures for wage assistance during the 3-year period. Only $24,000,000 of this amount was for the CWS program. Monthly expenditures for wage assistance under the CWA program reached their peak in January 1934 when they totaled almost $212,000,000. The decision of the Federal Government to terminate the Civil Works Administration and replace it with a program of work projects operated on a straight relief basis resulted in rapid liquidation of CWA activities and the transfer of a residual load of needy employees to the general relief rolls of the Federal Emergency Relief Administration. The drop in wage assistance payments for April 1934 and the immediate and subsequent rise in emergency relief expenditures mark this shift in administrative policy.

Works Program

The Works Program, authorized by the Federal Emergency Relief Act of 1935, was the third important wage assistance program of the Federal Government. It included within its scope the existing CCC program, as well as numerous other permanent and emergency units of the Federal Government. Most important of the new agencies was the Works Progress Administration, created to coordinate the entire employment program as well as to administer work projects. For purposes of the consolidated relief series, only WPA and CCC payments have been shown separately. Expenditures of all other agencies participating in the Works Program have been combined. The participating agencies are listed in appendix C.

The relief aspects of Works Program employment are clearly indicated by the enabling legislation and the rules and regulations governing eligibility and earnings. These require that preference in employment be given to able-bodied relief workers and that except where specific exemption is made a minimum of 90 percent of the employees

---

[34] Excludes earnings of persons employed on administrative projects. Includes hire paid to owner-drivers of teams, trucks, and mechanical equipment.

on any project be drawn from certified relief clients. Earnings for other than supervisory and administrative employees are set at a security level and vary in amount according to geographic location and class of work performed. Hourly wage rates are established for different regions with hours of work adjusted to permit employees to earn the monthly wage applicable to the type of work performed.[35]

Except for CCC payments wage assistance dispensed under the Works Program attained no considerable volume until August 1935. With the rapid transfer of employables from the emergency relief rolls, expenditures for wage assistance by WPA and other participating agencies mounted steadily, as shown by figure 17, while emergency relief expenditures gradually declined.[36] The net effect of these two movements on the total burden of public relief and assistance will appear from the combined trend shown later in this section.

Categorical Relief

During 1933, 1934, and 1935 relief to the aged, to the blind, and to dependent children was administered by State and local agencies operating outside the sphere of Federal financial or administrative control. Since there was no country-wide collection of monthly statistical data relating to categorical relief for this period,[37] monthly estimates of total expenditures for these types of aid have been prepared for this study from information available from miscellaneous sources. These sources are listed in appendix D, together with a description of the methods used in estimating the monthly expenditures for each category.

From the estimates it appears that approximately one-quarter of a billion dollars was expended in the United States during the 3-year period for relief to the aged, to the blind, and to dependent children. Of this total amount, the aged received about 48 percent, the blind 8 percent, and dependent children 44 percent. Estimated monthly expenditures for each class of relief are shown in table 22.

Combined expenditures for categorical relief, estimated at $34,920,000 for the first half of 1933, increased over the period approximately 70 percent to an estimated total of $59,440,000 during the second half of 1935. Most of this expansion occurred in old-age relief, which has constituted an increasing proportion of total expenditures for categorical relief. Estimated expenditures for this type of assist-

---

[35] Section 7 of the Emergency Relief Appropriation Act of 1935 conferred upon the President the right to fix such rates of pay as he believed would accomplish the purpose of the legislation and "not affect adversely or tend to decrease the going rates of wages paid for work of a similar nature." After June 1936 hourly earnings were determined in accordance with prevailing rates, in keeping with provisions of the Emergency Relief Act of 1936.

[36] See fig. 16, p. 66.

[37] See Part I, pp. 35–37, for data from the 120 urban areas included in the Urban Relief Series from 1929.

ance rose from $13,090,000 during the first half of 1933 to $35,940,000 during the second half of 1935, constituting 38 percent and 60 percent, respectively, of total categorical relief in the two periods. The enactment in a number of States of new laws providing aid to the aged accounts for the relatively large increase in this category.

The general expansion in categorical relief during 1935, which is indicated by the monthly estimates, is doubtless due in part to the anticipated operation of the Social Security Act, which was approved in August 1935 but did not function until January 1936, when the first grant was authorized.

THE COMBINED TREND OF PUBLIC ASSISTANCE

The combined trend of outdoor public assistance for the 36 months in 1933, 1934, and 1935 reveals marked fluctuations in total monthly expenditures as well as major changes in the amounts spent for the

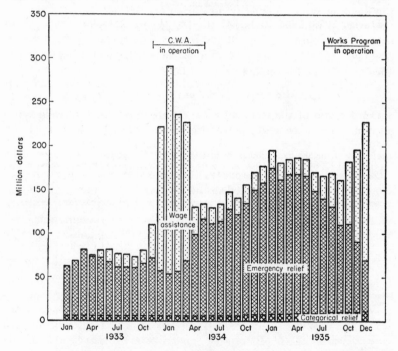

FIG. 18 – TREND OF MONTHLY EXPENDITURES FOR PUBLIC
RELIEF AND WAGE ASSISTANCE
IN THE UNITED STATES
January 1933 – December 1935

Source: Division of Research, Statistics, and Records,
Works Progress Administration. Estimates of categorical
relief based on miscellaneous sources listed in appendix D.   AF-1481, W.P.A.

component types of assistance. The changes in the relative importance of emergency relief, wage assistance, and categorical relief, shown in figure 18, are caused primarily by administrative shifts from one form of Federal assistance to another, resulting in changes in the type and level of assistance extended to needy individuals and families.

Effects of Administrative Shifts in Relief and Assistance Programs

Categorical relief was a relatively small and constant portion of outdoor public assistance during this period. The bulk of expenditures was for general emergency relief and wage assistance, with emphasis alternating between the two. Except during the comparatively brief period in which the Civil Works Administration was in operation and the period of Works Program development, emergency relief constituted the preponderant share of the total. Larger monthly payments extended under these two work programs explain in part the bulge in the combined trend during the winter of 1933–1934 and the upward movement during the latter part of 1935. The 3-year peak in expenditures occurred in January 1934, when the Civil Works program was at its height. Combined expenditures for public assistance in that month totaled $291,454,000.

Interdependence of Relief and Wage Assistance Trends

Comparison of the trend of total expenditures for the three types of public assistance with the trend of expenditures for categorical and

Table 23.—Monthly Expenditures for Emergency and Categorical Relief and for Emergency Relief, Categorical Relief, and Wage Assistance, Expressed as Relative Numbers,[1] Continental United States, January 1933–December 1935

[Average month 1933–1935=100 [2]]

Year and month	Emergency and categorical relief	Emergency relief, categorical relief, and wage assistance	Year and month	Emergency and categorical relief	Emergency relief, categorical relief, and wage assistance
1933			*1934*		
January	61	43	July	109	90
February	67	47	August	122	99
March	79	55	September	116	95
April	72	50	October	129	105
May	69	55	November	143	114
June	65	55	December	151	118
July	59	51			
August	60	51	*1935*		
September	58	49			
October	63	54	January	167	130
November	68	74	February	155	121
December	54	149	March	161	124
			April	161	125
1934			May	159	124
			June	142	114
January	52	195	July	134	111
February	55	158	August	125	113
March	66	152	September	106	108
April	95	87	October	107	123
May	111	90	November	87	132
June	106	86	December	67	154

[1] Rounded to the nearest unit.
[2] Base values are as follows: Emergency and categorical relief, $104,718,611; emergency relief, categorical relief, and wage assistance, $149,301,861.

emergency relief emphasizes the limitations of the relief series in Part I, which are exclusive of wage assistance. Obviously the trend of public expenditures for emergency relief was as significantly affected in these 3 years by the development of the wage assistance programs as by the impact of unemployment and drought. The months of lowest expenditure for categorical and emergency relief are the months of peak expenditure for all types of assistance combined. On the other hand, the months of peak expenditures for categorical and emergency relief are the months in which expenditures for wage assistance were comparatively small, thus tending to hold down the level of the combined series. The relative numbers shown in table 23 facilitate comparison of the trends of categorical and emergency relief and of total outdoor public assistance for the 36-month period.

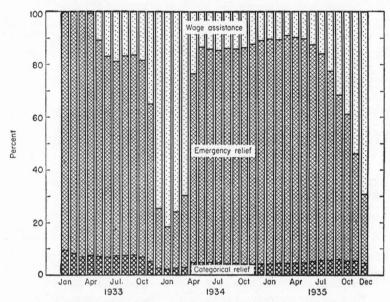

FIG. 19–PERCENT DISTRIBUTION OF MONTHLY EXPENDITURES
FOR PUBLIC RELIEF AND WAGE ASSISTANCE
IN THE UNITED STATES

January 1933–December 1935

Source: Division of Research, Statistics, and Records,
Works Progress Administration. Estimates of categorical
relief based on miscellaneous sources listed in appendix D.   AF-1483,W.P.A.

The interplay and reciprocal relationship between wage assistance and emergency relief is effectively illustrated by figure 19 which shows the relative rather than the absolute volume of expenditures for the three components of the public assistance structure over the 36 months. The percentage figures are given in table 24.

Table 24.—Percent Distribution [1] of Expenditures for Emergency Relief, Wage Assistance, and Categorical Relief, Continental United States, January 1933–December 1935

Year and month	Total public assistance	Emergency relief	Wage assistance	Categorical relief
1933				
January	100.0	90.6	—	9.4
February	100.0	91.6	—	8.4
March	100.0	92.9	—	7.1
April	100.0	92.2	0.1	7.7
May	100.0	82.2	10.7	7.1
June	100.0	76.1	17.0	6.9
July	100.0	73.8	18.8	7.4
August	100.0	75.8	16.7	7.5
September	100.0	75.7	16.5	7.8
October	100.0	74.6	18.4	7.0
November	100.0	60.0	34.8	5.2
December	100.0	22.9	74.5	2.6
1934				
January	100.0	16.6	81.4	2.0
February	100.0	21.7	75.8	2.5
March	100.0	27.5	69.8	2.7
April	100.0	71.9	23.4	4.7
May	100.0	82.0	13.3	4.7
June	100.0	81.0	14.1	4.9
July	100.0	80.8	14.4	4.8
August	100.0	82.0	13.7	4.3
September	100.0	81.5	13.9	4.6
October	100.0	82.2	13.6	4.2
November	100.0	84.1	11.9	4.0
December	100.0	85.2	10.6	4.2
1935				
January	100.0	85.8	10.0	4.2
February	100.0	85.1	10.4	4.5
March	100.0	86.5	8.9	4.6
April	100.0	85.6	9.7	4.7
May	100.0	85.2	10.0	4.8
June	100.0	82.2	12.5	5.3
July	100.0	78.8	15.6	5.6
August	100.0	72.0	22.3	5.7
September	100.0	62.4	31.6	6.0
October	100.0	55.5	39.0	5.5
November	100.0	40.9	53.9	5.2
December	100.0	26.1	69.3	4.6

[1] For absolute figures upon which these percentages are based, see table 22.

Emergency relief constituted more than 90 percent of total expenditures for outdoor public assistance in January 1933, at which time wage assistance was nonexistent. By January 1934, emergency relief had dwindled to 17 percent of the monthly total while wage assistance had risen to 81 percent. Emergency relief again accounted for the major share of expenditures in January 1935, with wage assistance only 10 percent of the total. With the initiation of the Works Program in the latter half of 1935 emergency relief began to decrease and wage assistance to increase in relative importance.

VARIABILITY IN UNDERLYING STATE TRENDS

The consolidated relief and wage assistance series which has been constructed provides a measure of the trend of expenditures in the total United States. The development of consolidated relief and assistance series for the separate States and localities has not been attempted in this report but it is certain that if such series were built up they would show wide variability. Evidence of such variability among the States is supplied by the charts at the end of the report, which trace for the general relief program only the trends of obligations incurred for relief extended to cases and of cases receiving relief in the United States, in nine geographic divisions and in the individual States, from July 1933 through December 1935.[38] The data charted here represent the largest component element in any consolidated series for the respective areas in these 3 years. The span of active operation of the Civil Works Administration and of the Works Program within the period covered is indicated by cross-hatching of the background. This cross-hatching serves two useful purposes: it flags the major cause of the decline in the volume of emergency relief operations occurring in these two periods and it calls attention to differences among the divisions and States in the timing of the impact of the wage-assistance programs.

Further evidence of the variability in State relief patterns, which would be reflected in State or local consolidated series, is supplied by figures 21, 22, and 23. These charts, all constructed on the same general principle, provide three sets of State comparisons for the general relief program at half-yearly intervals from July 1933 through July 1935. The first chart relates to obligations incurred for relief per inhabitant; the second, to the percent of population on relief; and the third, to average relief benefits per family case.[39] The figures upon which the charts are based are presented, together with figures for additional months, in appendix tables 8, 9, and 10.

In the development of State and local consolidated series, some technical problems arise which are not a source of difficulty in the construction of a national series. For example, wage assistance extended by the Civilian Conservation Corps cannot be measured locally. Employees on this program are commonly assigned to camps which are not located in their place of residence, and statistics are not compiled according to residence. To a lesser degree, this same problem arises in connection with other wage assistance programs: employees on projects do not necessarily work in the locality in which they reside. A similar problem is presented by transient relief which probably should be excluded from any local series.

---

[38] Fig. 20, pp. 81–86. As a preliminary to constructing the charts the data for both cases and obligations incurred were plotted on a semilogarithmic or ratio background. Through each curve a horizontal base line was drawn representing the average month in the second half of 1933. The obligation and case curves for each area were then paired by superimposing the base lines. Rates of changes in cases and in obligations from this base period can therefore be readily compared.

[39] In each chart individual States are represented by numbered circles. The States are arrayed in each month according to the size of the rate or average. The arrow in each column points to the median, while the shaded area marks off the interquartile range. Approximately one-half of the States fall within this area, one-fourth above, and one-fourth below the median value. States falling either above or below the shaded area may be considered to represent extreme situations.

EXTENSION OF THE PROPOSED INTEGRATED SERIES BEYOND 1935

The pattern which has been developed here for an integrated relief and wage assistance series is considered experimental rather than definitive. It has been set up as much with a view to stimulating discussion as for the purpose of establishing a complete measure of the volume and trend of public assistance in the last 3 years of the 26-year period covered by this report. Although the series has not been extended beyond 1935 it lays a foundation for a national series to be currently posted. Extension of the series into 1936 would, of course, show radical changes in emphasis on the three component types of assistance. Expenditures for wage assistance expanded markedly with the further development of the Works Program, and emergency relief expenditures contracted with the return of direct relief to the States and localities. Categorical relief has increased under the stimulus of new legislation and the grants-in-aid provided by the Social Security Act.

Monthly data on categorical relief, which were estimated for 1933, 1934, and 1935, have been collected currently by the Social Security Board since the beginning of 1936. Because of the decentralization of general relief administration in 1936, which resulted from the withdrawal of the Federal Government from the support of emergency relief, monthly data reported for general outdoor (emergency) relief in 1936 are not fully comparable for all States with those for earlier years. This would necessarily result in some weakening of a national integrated series. In many States, however, the comparability of the data has not been impaired. This fact emphasizes the desirability of State and local series to supplement any national series.

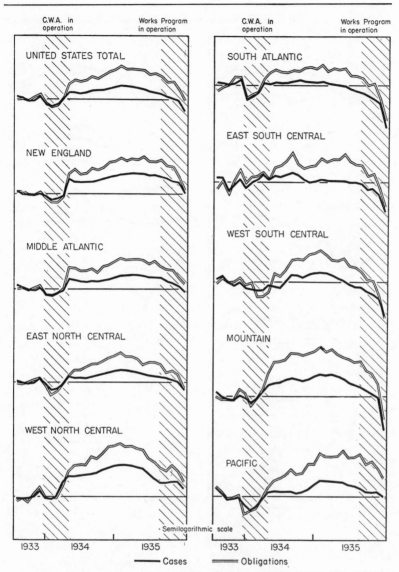

FIG. 20 - TRENDS OF RELIEF CASES AND OF OBLIGATIONS INCURRED
FOR RELIEF EXTENDED TO CASES

General Relief Program, as Reported to the F.E.R.A.

July 1933 – December 1935

Note: The horizontal line running through each pair of curves
represents the average month, July to December 1933,
for both cases and obligations.

Source: Division of Research, Statistics, and Records, Works Progress Administration.

AF-1171, W.P.A.

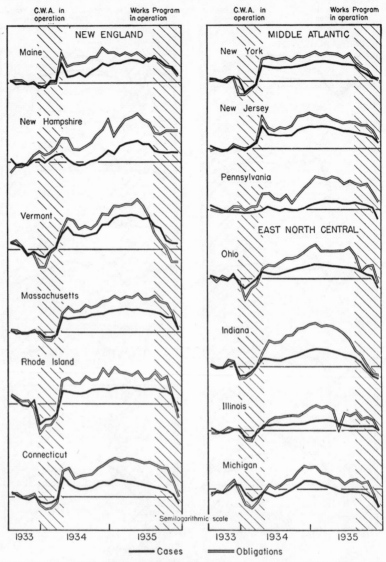

FIG. 20 - TRENDS OF RELIEF CASES AND OF OBLIGATIONS INCURRED
FOR RELIEF EXTENDED TO CASES

General Relief Program, as Reported to the F.E.R.A.

July 1933 - December 1935

— Continued —

Note: The horizontal line running through each pair of curves
represents the average month, July to December 1933,
for both cases and obligations.

Source: Division of Research, Statistics, and Records, Works Progress Administration.

AF-1171, W.P.A.

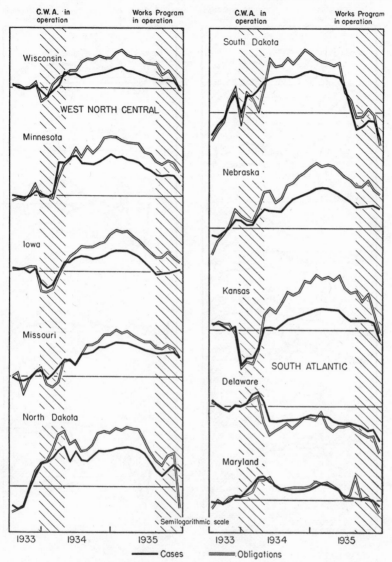

FIG. 20- TRENDS OF RELIEF CASES AND OF OBLIGATIONS INCURRED
FOR RELIEF EXTENDED TO CASES
General Relief Program, as Reported to the F.E.R.A.
July 1933 – December 1935
— Continued —

Note: The horizontal line running through each pair of curves
represents the average month, July to December 1933,
for both cases and obligations.

Source: Division of Research, Statistics, and Records, Works Progress Administration.   AF-1171, W.P.A.

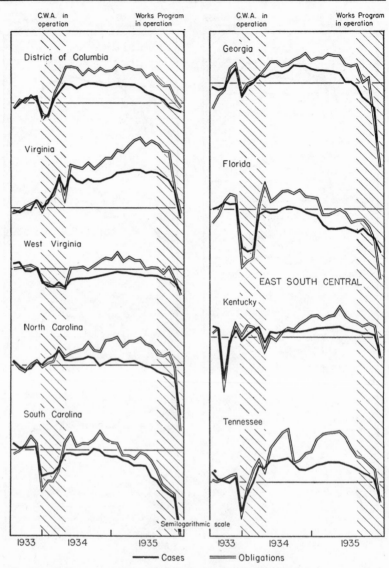

C.W.A. in operation   Works Program in operation   C.W.A. in operation   Works Program in operation

District of Columbia

Georgia

Virginia

Florida

West Virginia

EAST SOUTH CENTRAL

Kentucky

North Carolina

South Carolina

Tennessee

Semilogarithmic scale

1933   1934   1935   1933   1934   1935

——— Cases   ═══ Obligations

FIG. 20 - TRENDS OF RELIEF CASES AND OF OBLIGATIONS INCURRED
FOR RELIEF EXTENDED TO CASES
General Relief Program, as Reported to the F.E.R.A.
July 1933 - December 1935
— Continued —

Note: The horizontal line running through each pair of curves
represents the average month, July to December 1933,
for both cases and obligations.

Source: Division of Research, Statistics, and Records, Works Progress Administration.

AF-1171, W.P.A.

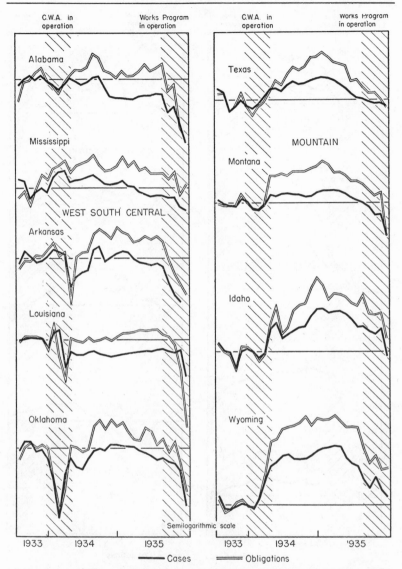

FIG. 20 - TRENDS OF RELIEF CASES AND OF OBLIGATIONS INCURRED
FOR RELIEF EXTENDED TO CASES
General Relief Program, as Reported to the F.E.R.A.
July 1933 – December 1935
— Continued —

Note: The horizontal line running through each pair of curves
represents the average month, July to December 1933,
for both cases and obligations.

Source: Division of Research, Statistics, and Records, Works Progress Administration.   AF–1171, W.P.A.

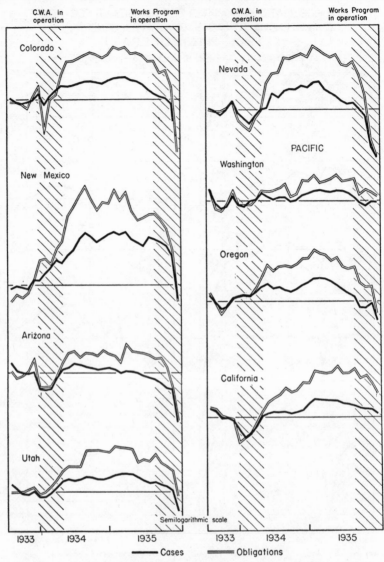

FIG. 20-TRENDS OF RELIEF CASES AND OF OBLIGATIONS INCURRED
FOR RELIEF EXTENDED TO CASES

General Relief Program, as Reported to the F.E.R.A.

July 1933 – December 1935

— Continued —

Note: The horizontal line running through each pair of curves
represents the average month, July to December 1933,
for both cases and obligations.

Source: Division of Research, Statistics, and Records, Works Progress Administration.

AF-1171, W.P.A.

FIG. 21 – OBLIGATIONS INCURRED PER INHABITANT FOR RELIEF
EXTENDED TO CASES, BY STATES, GENERAL
RELIEF PROGRAM, F.E.R.A.

HALF-YEARLY INTERVALS, JULY 1933 – JULY 1935

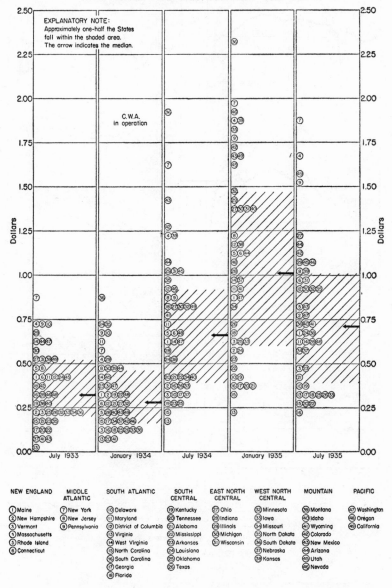

EXPLANATORY NOTE:
Approximately one-half the States
fall within the shaded area.
The arrow indicates the median.

C.W.A.
in operation

NEW ENGLAND	MIDDLE ATLANTIC	SOUTH ATLANTIC	SOUTH CENTRAL	EAST NORTH CENTRAL	WEST NORTH CENTRAL	MOUNTAIN	PACIFIC
① Maine	⑦ New York	⑩ Delaware	⑲ Kentucky	㉗ Ohio	㉜ Minnesota	㊴ Montana	㊼ Washington
② New Hampshire	⑧ New Jersey	⑪ Maryland	⑳ Tennessee	㉘ Indiana	㉝ Iowa	㊵ Idaho	㊽ Oregon
③ Vermont	⑨ Pennsylvania	⑫ District of Columbia	㉑ Alabama	㉙ Illinois	㉞ Missouri	㊶ Wyoming	㊾ California
④ Massachusetts		⑬ Virginia	㉒ Mississippi	㉚ Michigan	㉟ North Dakota	㊷ Colorado	
⑤ Rhode Island		⑭ West Virginia	㉓ Arkansas	㉛ Wisconsin	㊱ South Dakota	㊸ New Mexico	
⑥ Connecticut		⑮ North Carolina	㉔ Louisiana		㊲ Nebraska	㊹ Arizona	
		⑯ South Carolina	㉕ Oklahoma		㊳ Kansas	㊺ Utah	
		⑰ Georgia	㉖ Texas			㊻ Nevada	
		⑱ Florida					

Source: Division of Research, Statistics, and Records, Works Progress Administration

AF-1017, W.P.A.

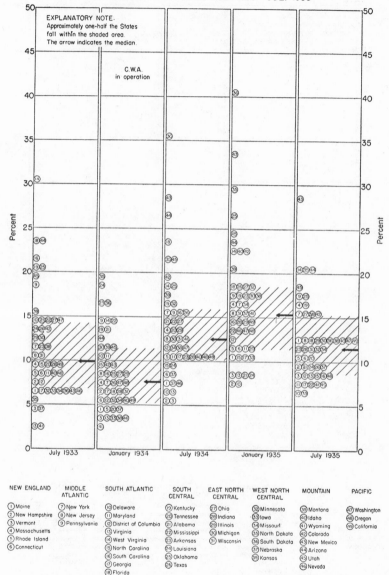

FIG. 22 – PERCENT OF POPULATION RECEIVING RELIEF, BY
STATES, GENERAL RELIEF PROGRAM,
F.E.R.A.

HALF-YEARLY INTERVALS, JULY 1933 – JULY 1935

EXPLANATORY NOTE.
Approximately one-half the States
fall within the shaded area.
The arrow indicates the median.

C.W.A.
in operation

NEW ENGLAND	MIDDLE ATLANTIC	SOUTH ATLANTIC	SOUTH CENTRAL	EAST NORTH CENTRAL	WEST NORTH CENTRAL	MOUNTAIN	PACIFIC
① Maine	⑦ New York	⑩ Delaware	⑲ Kentucky	㉗ Ohio	㉜ Minnesota	㊴ Montana	㊼ Washington
② New Hampshire	⑧ New Jersey	⑪ Maryland	⑳ Tennessee	㉘ Indiana	㉝ Iowa	㊵ Idaho	㊽ Oregon
③ Vermont	⑨ Pennsylvania	⑫ District of Columbia	㉑ Alabama	㉙ Illinois	㉞ Missouri	㊶ Wyoming	㊾ California
④ Massachusetts		⑬ Virginia	㉒ Mississippi	㉚ Michigan	㉟ North Dakota	㊷ Colorado	
⑤ Rhode Island		⑭ West Virginia	㉓ Arkansas	㉛ Wisconsin	㊱ South Dakota	㊸ New Mexico	
⑥ Connecticut		⑮ North Carolina	㉔ Louisiana		㊲ Nebraska	㊹ Arizona	
		⑯ South Carolina	㉕ Oklahoma		㊳ Kansas	㊺ Utah	
		⑰ Georgia	㉖ Texas			㊻ Nevada	
		⑱ Florida					

Source: Division of Research, Statistics, and Records, Works Progress Administration

AF – 1015, W.P.A.

FIG. 23–AVERAGE MONTHLY RELIEF BENEFIT PER FAMILY CASE,
BY STATES, GENERAL RELIEF PROGRAM,
F.E.R.A.

HALF-YEARLY INTERVALS, JULY 1933 – JULY 1935

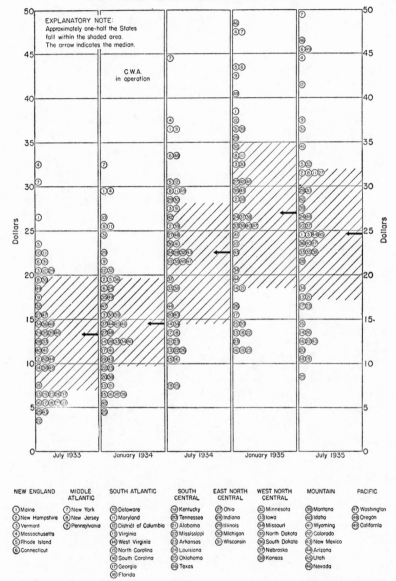

EXPLANATORY NOTE:
Approximately one-half the States
fall within the shaded area.
The arrow indicates the median.

C.W.A.
in operation

NEW ENGLAND	MIDDLE ATLANTIC	SOUTH ATLANTIC	SOUTH CENTRAL	EAST NORTH CENTRAL	WEST NORTH CENTRAL	MOUNTAIN	PACIFIC
① Maine	⑦ New York	⑩ Delaware	⑲ Kentucky	㉗ Ohio	㉜ Minnesota	㊴ Montana	㊼ Washington
② New Hampshire	⑧ New Jersey	⑪ Maryland	⑳ Tennessee	㉘ Indiana	㉝ Iowa	㊵ Idaho	㊽ Oregon
③ Vermont	⑨ Pennsylvania	⑫ District of Columbia	㉑ Alabama	㉙ Illinois	㉞ Missouri	㊶ Wyoming	㊾ California
④ Massachusetts		⑬ Virginia	㉒ Mississippi	㉚ Michigan	㉟ North Dakota	㊷ Colorado	
⑤ Rhode Island		⑭ West Virginia	㉓ Arkansas	㉛ Wisconsin	㊱ South Dakota	㊸ New Mexico	
⑥ Connecticut		⑮ North Carolina	㉔ Louisiana		㊲ Nebraska	㊹ Arizona	
		⑯ South Carolina	㉕ Oklahoma		㊳ Kansas	㊺ Utah	
		⑰ Georgia	㉖ Texas			㊻ Nevada	
		⑱ Florida					

Source: Division of Research, Statistics, and Records, Works Progress Administration

AF–1019, W.P.A.

Appendix A

SUPPLEMENTARY TABLES

Table 1.—Year of Original Enactment of State Legislation for Categorical Relief and for Emergency Unemployment Relief, as of December 31, 1935

State and geographic division	Categorical relief			Emergency unemployment relief [4]
	Aid to the aged [1]	Aid to the blind [2]	Aid to dependent children [3]	
New England:				
Maine	1933	1915	1917	1935
New Hampshire	1931	1915	1913	1931
Vermont	1935	1935	1917	—
Massachusetts	1930	[5]1920	1913	1931
Rhode Island	1935	—	1923	1931
Connecticut	1935	[5]1921	1919	1931
Middle Atlantic:				
New York	1930	1922	1915	1931
New Jersey	1931	1931	1913	1931
Pennsylvania	1933	1933	1913	1931
East North Central:				
Ohio	1933	1898	1913	1931
Indiana	1933	1935	1919	1931
Illinois	1935	1903	1911	1932
Michigan	1933	—	1913	1933
Wisconsin	1925	1907	1913	1932
West North Central:				
Minnesota	1929	1913	1913	1931
Iowa	1934	1915	1913	1934
Missouri	1935	1923	[6]1917	1933
North Dakota	1933	—	1915	1933
South Dakota	—	—	1913	1933
Nebraska	1933	1917	1913	1933
Kansas	—	1911	1915	1933
South Atlantic:				
Delaware	1931	—	1917	1932
Maryland	1927	1929	1916	1931
District of Columbia	1935	1935	1926	—
Virginia	—	—	1918	—
West Virginia	1931	—	1915	1931
North Carolina	—	—	1923	—
South Carolina	—	—	—	—
Georgia	—	—	—	—
Florida	1935	1935	1919	1935
East South Central:				
Kentucky	1926	1924	1928	1933
Tennessee	—	—	1915	1933
Alabama	1935	—	—	1932
Mississippi	1934	1935	1928	1935

[1] Data from Bureau of Labor Statistics, Parker, Florence E., "Experience Under State Old-Age Pension Acts in 1934," *Monthly Labor Review*, August 1935, pp. 303–305. Information on laws enacted during remainder of 1935 supplied by Bureau.

[2] Data from Bureau of Labor Statistics, "Public Pensions for the Blind in 1935," *Monthly Labor Review*, August 1936, pp. 305–307.

[3] Data from U. S. Children's Bureau, Chart No. 3, "A Tabular Summary of State Laws Relating to Public Aid to Children in Their Own Homes in Effect January 1, 1934."

[4] The dates given are for the first State legislation financing emergency unemployment relief. Acts creating emergency relief administrative bodies or authorizing investigations are omitted unless involving financial aid. Data from Lowe, Robert C., *FERA Digest of State Legislation for the Financing of Emergency Relief, January 1, 1931–June 30, 1935*, Municipal Finance Section, Federal Emergency Relief Administration, August 1, 1935; and Lowe, Robert C. and Staff, *Supplement for Period July 1, 1935–February 29, 1936*, Division of Social Research, Works Progress Administration, 1936.

[5] Year in which blind pension provision was added to act.

[6] In 1911 a State law was enacted authorizing aid to dependent children in Jackson and St. Louis Counties.

Table 1.—Year of Original Enactment of State Legislation for Categorical Relief and for Emergency Unemployment Relief, as of December 31, 1935—Continued

State and geographic division	Categorical relief			Emergency unemployment relief
	Aid to the aged	Aid to the blind	Aid to dependent children	
West South Central:				
Arkansas	1935	1931	1917	1935
Louisiana	—	1928	1920	1934
Oklahoma	1935	1935	1915	1931
Texas	—	—	1917	1933
Mountain:				
Montana	1923	—	1915	1933
Idaho	1931	1917	1913	1935
Wyoming	1929	1935	1915	1933
Colorado	1927	1925	1913	1933
New Mexico	—	—	1931	1935
Arizona	1933	—	[7] 1914	1933
Utah	1929	1931	1913	1933
Nevada	[8] 1923	1925	1913	1933
Pacific:				
Washington	1933	1933	1913	1933
Oregon	1933	1935	1913	1933
California	1929	1929	1913	1931

[7] Declared unconstitutional; next act passed 1917.
[8] Repealed same year; next act passed 1925.

Source: Compiled from miscellaneous sources listed in footnotes.

Table 2.—Expenditures for Relief to Families in Their Homes and to Homeless Men in 308 Cities, by States, First Quarters of 1929 and of 1931, With Percent From Governmental and Private Funds and Percent of Change Between 1929 and 1931

State and geographic division	Number of cities reporting	Total expenditures first quarter		Percent				Percent of change from first quarter of 1929 to first quarter of 1931		
				Governmental		Private				
				First quarter		First quarter				
		1929	1931	1929	1931	1929	1931	Total	Governmental	Private
Total	308	$16,621,341	$56,669,124	65.0	60.4	35.0	39.6	240.9	216.6	286.1
New England	44	3,099,842	7,584,543	81.7	86.6	18.3	13.4	144.7	159.5	78.6
Maine	2	85,150	107,667	95.5	91.9	4.5	8.1	26.4	21.7	127.4
New Hampshire	2	38,814	71,797	94.2	88.7	5.8	11.3	85.0	74.1	262.7
Vermont [1]	—	—	—	—	—	—	—	—	—	—
Massachusetts	29	2,504,217	5,469,708	87.1	90.6	12.9	9.4	118.4	127.2	59.4
Rhode Island [2]	3	118,457	343,502	66.2	53.4	33.8	46.6	190.0	133.8	300.2
Connecticut	8	353,204	1,591,869	43.6	79.7	56.4	20.3	350.7	723.3	62.2
Middle Atlantic	64	5,611,877	21,250,354	67.7	46.2	32.3	53.8	278.7	158.6	529.9
New York	22	3,835,797	15,131,933	71.2	51.3	28.8	48.7	294.5	184.4	566.9
New Jersey	22	553,096	1,775,322	80.8	69.6	19.2	30.4	221.0	176.5	408.1
Pennsylvania	20	1,222,984	4,343,099	50.6	18.8	49.4	81.2	255.1	31.8	483.7
East North Central	81	3,877,753	17,934,510	66.0	68.3	34.0	31.7	362.5	378.7	331.0
Ohio	23	1,187,575	3,433,126	45.8	36.2	54.2	63.8	189.1	128.7	240.1
Indiana	13	244,976	1,338,451	51.5	71.3	48.5	28.7	446.4	657.3	222.7
Illinois	20	1,012,381	4,135,889	64.1	35.1	35.9	64.9	308.5	123.7	638.0
Michigan	15	1,035,036	7,289,698	88.0	96.6	12.0	3.4	604.3	672.5	101.7
Wisconsin	10	397,785	1,737,346	82.8	89.9	17.2	10.1	336.8	374.0	156.9

[1] No incorporated areas of over 30,000 in this State
[2] No report from Pawtucket.

Table 2.—Expenditures for Relief to Families in Their Homes and to Homeless Men in 308 Cities, by States, First Quarters of 1929 and 1931, With Percent From Governmental and Private Funds and Percent of Change Between 1929 and 1931—Continued

State and geographic division	Number of cities reporting	Total expenditures first quarter		Percent				Percent of change from first quarter of 1929 to first quarter of 1931		
				Governmental First quarter		Private First quarter				
		1929	1931	1929	1931	1929	1931	Total	Governmental	Private
West North Central	21	$1,142,443	$2,219,126	49.5	49.6	50.5	50.4	94.2	94.7	93.8
Minnesota	3	435,000	728,472	58.5	57.7	41.5	42.3	67.5	65.2	70.7
Iowa	7	180,019	326,610	66.2	56.8	33.8	43.2	81.4	55.5	132.8
Missouri	5	365,764	919,875	24.6	39.0	75.4	61.0	151.5	299.4	103.3
North Dakota [1]	—	—	—	—	—	—	—	—	—	—
South Dakota	1	14,887	12,914	94.0	93.6	6.0	6.4	−13.3	−13.6	−8.0
Nebraska	2	77,317	115,628	51.4	45.8	48.6	54.2	49.6	33.4	66.7
Kansas	3	69,456	115,627	69.5	61.4	30.5	38.6	66.5	47.1	110.6
South Atlantic	34	587,031	1,406,687	27.2	25.8	72.8	74.2	139.6	128.1	143.9
Delaware	1	13,711	198,618	—	5.0	100.0	95.0	1,348.6	—	1,276.1
Maryland	3	135,196	378,394	12.7	32.6	87.3	67.4	179.9	616.4	116.2
District of Columbia	1	89,894	188,873	39.9	21.1	60.1	78.9	110.1	11.1	175.9
Virginia	6	92,985	140,755	14.1	16.7	85.9	83.3	51.4	78.9	46.9
West Virginia	3	46,577	113,730	50.4	32.3	49.6	67.7	144.2	56.5	233.3
North Carolina	8	72,409	145,956	26.7	29.0	73.3	71.0	101.6	119.0	95.2
South Carolina	2	20,716	28,250	24.2	27.6	75.8	72.4	36.4	55.7	30.2
Georgia	5	44,036	118,660	8.2	22.0	91.8	78.0	169.5	625.8	129.0
Florida	5	71,507	93,451	58.4	57.7	41.6	42.3	30.7	29.2	32.8
East South Central	13	213,666	695,418	18.6	39.4	81.4	60.6	225.5	589.1	142.4
Kentucky	4	78,571	272,192	19.9	53.2	80.1	46.8	246.4	826.8	102.3
Tennessee	4	90,651	238,893	26.5	22.4	73.5	77.6	163.5	122.8	178.2
Alabama	3	39,897	171,232	—	43.6	100.0	56.4	329.4	—	142.2
Mississippi	2	4,547	13,001	2.5	6.0	97.5	94.0	185.9	582.5	175.7
West South Central	21	280,539	866,156	30.9	45.3	69.1	54.7	208.7	352.4	144.5
Arkansas	2	22,991	104,790	21.0	55.8	79.0	44.2	355.8	1,113.7	154.8
Louisiana	3	33,704	60,381	1.8	1.5	98.2	98.5	79.2	47.0	79.7
Oklahoma	3	80,624	359,713	55.2	55.9	44.8	44.1	346.2	352.2	338.7
Texas	13	143,220	341,272	25.7	38.6	74.3	61.4	138.3	258.0	96.9
Mountain	8	269,111	447,477	71.8	67.8	28.2	32.2	66.3	57.2	89.4
Montana	1	33,427	54,492	93.9	76.6	6.1	23.4	63.0	33.1	520.8
Idaho [1]	—	—	—	—	—	—	—	—	—	—
Wyoming [1]	—	—	—	—	—	—	—	—	—	—
Colorado	3	155,081	201,815	70.6	74.1	29.4	25.9	30.1	36.6	14.6
New Mexico [1]	—	—	—	—	—	—	—	—	—	—
Arizona	2	24,316	48,013	42.8	37.8	57.2	62.2	97.5	74.3	114.7
Utah	2	56,287	143,157	74.4	65.8	25.6	34.2	154.3	124.9	239.8
Nevada [1]	—	—	—	—	—	—	—	—	—	—
Pacific	22	1,539,079	4,264,853	56.5	73.3	43.5	26.7	177.1	259.6	70.0
Washington	5	267,504	521,569	49.0	53.9	51.0	46.1	95.0	114.3	76.4
Oregon	1	91,981	399,052	44.1	76.6	55.9	23.4	333.8	652.3	82.1
California [3]	16	1,179,594	3,344,232	59.1	75.9	40.9	24.1	183.5	264.1	66.9

[1] No incorporated areas of over 30,000 in this State.
[3] No report from Santa Ana.

Source: U. S. Department of Commerce, Bureau of the Census, special report, *Relief Expenditures by Governmental and Private Organizations, 1929 and 1931*, 1932.

Table 3.—Expenditures per Inhabitant for Relief to Families in Their Homes and to Homeless Men in 308 Cities, by States, First Quarters of 1929 and of 1931

State and geographic division	Number of cities reporting	Total		Governmental		Private	
		First quarter		First quarter		First quarter	
		1929	1931	1929	1931	1929	1931
Total	308	$0.34	$1.17	$0.22	$0.71	$0.12	$0.46
New England	44	.75	1.85	.61	1.60	.14	.25
Maine	2	.81	1.02	.77	.94	.04	.08
New Hampshire	2	.36	.66	.34	.59	.02	.07
Vermont [1]	—	—	—	—	—	—	—
Massachusetts	29	.90	1.96	.78	1.78	.12	.18
Rhode Island [2]	3	.34	.99	.23	.53	.11	.46
Connecticut	8	.46	2.09	.20	1.66	.26	.43
Middle Atlantic	64	.36	1.37	.24	.63	.12	.74
New York	22	.42	1.65	.30	.85	.12	.80
New Jersey	22	.26	.83	.21	.58	.05	.25
Pennsylvania	20	.29	1.03	.15	.19	.14	.84
East North Central	81	.31	1.43	.20	.98	.11	.45
Ohio	23	.36	1.04	.16	.38	.20	.66
Indiana	13	.20	1.10	.10	.79	.10	.31
Illinois	20	.23	.94	.15	.33	.08	.61
Michigan	15	.41	2.86	.36	2.76	.05	.10
Wisconsin	10	.36	1.59	.30	1.43	.06	.16
West North Central	21	.34	.67	.17	.33	.17	.34
Minnesota	3	.52	.87	.30	.50	.22	.37
Iowa	7	.38	.70	.25	.40	.13	.30
Missouri	5	.26	.66	.06	.26	.20	.40
North Dakota [1]	—	—	—	—	—	—	—
South Dakota	1	.45	.39	.42	.36	.03	.03
Nebraska	2	.27	.40	.14	.18	.13	.22
Kansas	3	.23	.39	.16	.24	.07	.15
South Atlantic	34	.16	.39	.04	.10	.12	.29
Delaware	1	.13	1.86	—	.09	.13	1.77
Maryland	3	.15	.43	.02	.14	.13	.29
District of Columbia	1	.18	.39	.07	.08	.11	.31
Virginia	6	.19	.28	.03	.05	.16	.23
West Virginia	3	.24	.58	.12	.19	.12	.39
North Carolina	8	.18	.35	.05	.10	.13	.25
South Carolina	2	.18	.25	.04	.07	.14	.18
Georgia	5	.09	.23	.01	.05	.08	18
Florida	5	.17	.23	.10	.13	.07	.10
East South Central	13	.14	.45	.03	.18	.11	.27
Kentucky	4	.17	.60	.03	.32	.14	.28
Tennessee	4	.14	.38	.04	.08	.10	.30
Alabama	3	.10	.43	—	.19	.10	.24
Mississippi	2	.06	.16	[3]	.01	.06	.15
West South Central	21	.11	.35	.03	.16	.08	.19
Arkansas	2	.20	.93	.04	.52	.16	.41
Louisiana	3	.06	.11	[3]	[3]	.06	.11
Oklahoma	3	.22	1.00	.12	.56	.10	.44
Texas	13	.10	.24	.03	.09	.07	.15
Mountain	8	.40	.67	.29	.45	.11	.22
Montana	1	.84	1.38	.79	1.06	.05	.32
Idaho [1]	—	—	—	—	—	—	—
Wyoming [1]	—	—	—	—	—	—	—
Colorado	3	.42	.54	.30	.40	.12	.14
New Mexico [1]	—	—	—	—	—	—	—
Arizona	2	.30	.60	.13	.23	.17	.37
Utah	2	.31	.79	.23	.52	.08	.27
Nevada [1]	—	—	—	—	—	—	—
Pacific	22	.33	.91	.19	.67	.14	.24
Washington	5	.41	.80	.20	.43	.21	.37
Oregon	1	.30	1.32	.13	1.01	.17	.31
California [4]	16	.32	.90	.19	.68	.13	.22

[1] No incorporated areas of over 30,000 in this State.
[2] No report from Pawtucket.
[3] Less than $0.005.
[4] No report from Santa Ana.

Source: U. S. Department of Commerce, Bureau of the Census, special report, *Relief Expenditures by Governmental and Private Organizations, 1929 and 1931*, 1932.

Table 4.—Cities Represented in Urban Relief Series, U. S. Children's Bureau

State and city

Alabama:	Massachusetts:	Ohio—Continued
Birmingham	Boston	Springfield
Mobile	Brockton	Toledo
California:	Cambridge	Youngstown
Berkeley	Fall River	Oklahoma:
Los Angeles	Lawrence	Tulsa
Oakland	Lowell	Oregon:
Sacramento	Lynn	Portland
San Diego	Malden	Pennsylvania:
San Francisco	New Bedford	Allentown
Colorado:	Newton	Altoona
Denver	Springfield	Bethlehem
Connecticut:	Worcester	Chester
Bridgeport	Michigan:	Erie
Hartford	Detroit	Harrisburg
New Britain	Flint	Johnstown
New Haven	Grand Rapids	Lancaster
Delaware:	Pontiac	Philadelphia
Wilmington	Saginaw	Pittsburgh
District of Columbia:	Minnesota:	Reading
Washington	Duluth	Scranton
Florida:	Minneapolis	Sharon
Jacksonville	St. Paul	Wilkes-Barre
Miami	Missouri:	Rhode Island:
Georgia:	Kansas City	Providence
Atlanta	St. Louis	So h Carolina:
Illinois:	Nebraska:	'harleston
Chicago	Omaha	Te essee:
Springfield	New Jersey:	Knoxville
Indiana:	Jersey City	Memphis
Evansville	Newark	Nashville
Fort Wayne	Trenton	Texas:
Indianapolis	New York:	Dallas
South Bend	Albany	El Paso
Terre Haute	Buffalo	Fort Worth
Iowa:	New Rochelle	Houston
Des Moines	New York	San Antonio
Sioux City	Niagara Falls	Utah:
Kansas:	Rochester	Salt Lake City
Kansas City	Syracuse	Virginia:
Topeka	Utica	Norfolk
Wichita	Yonkers	Richmond
Kentucky:	North Carolina:	Roanoke
Louisville	Asheville	Washington:
Louisiana:	Charlotte	Seattle
New Orleans	Greensboro	Tacoma
Shreveport	Winston-Salem	West Virginia:
Maine:	Ohio:	Huntington
Portland	Akron	Wisconsin:
Maryland:	Canton	Kenosha
Baltimore	Cincinnati	Madison
	Cleveland	Milwaukee
	Columbus	Racine
	Dayton	

Source: Winslow, Emma A., *Trends in Different Types of Public and Private Relief in Urban Areas, 1929–35*, Publication No. 237, U. S. Department of Labor, Children's Bureau, 1937.

Table 5.—Monthly Expenditures for Relief From Public and Private Funds in 120 Urban Areas, Expressed as Relative Numbers, January 1929–December 1935 [1]

[Average month 1931–1933=100 [2]]

Year and month	Total public and private	Public			Total private
		Total	General	Special allowances	
1929					
January	14.9	13.0	7.1	46.5	26.3
February	14.9	13.1	7.3	45.8	26.0
March	15.0	13.2	7.3	46.9	25.5
April	14.0	12.5	6.5	46.7	22.9
May	13.5	12.2	6.0	47.3	21.4
June	12.8	11.7	5.5	46.9	19.8
July	12.7	11.5	5.4	46.8	19.8
August	12.8	11.6	5.4	47.3	19.5
September	12.6	11.5	5.3	47.0	19.4
October	13.5	12.3	6.1	47.7	20.9
November	14.7	13.3	7.2	47.6	23.0
December	17.9	15.6	9.8	48.7	31.3
1930					
January	20.0	18.0	12.4	50.3	31.8
February	20.4	18.7	13.1	50.5	30.9
March	21.9	20.2	14.7	52.1	31.5
April	21.2	19.5	13.8	52.0	31.0
May	19.2	17.6	11.4	52.7	29.2
June	18.1	16.5	10.1	53.2	27.3
July	18.1	16.7	10.1	54.5	26.4
August	18.6	17.5	11.0	54.5	25.6
September	19.8	18.7	12.4	55.1	26.3
October	23.0	22.0	16.1	55.8	28.9
November	28.3	25.8	20.5	56.4	42.5
December	47.9	36.5	32.6	58.6	115.2
1931					
January	55.6	42.5	37.2	72.7	132.9
February	58.6	43.5	38.0	75.0	147.8
March	64.7	47.3	41.5	80.2	167.8
April	55.5	43.3	36.4	82.8	127.8
May	51.2	44.4	37.2	85.9	91.6
June	47.7	43.9	36.1	88.3	70.0
July	46.8	44.6	36.5	90.6	59.9
August	43.1	40.6	31.7	91.6	57.8
September	45.5	42.8	34.0	93.2	61.7
October	50.4	46.2	37.6	95.5	75.3
November	61.0	52.1	44.2	97.5	113.5
December	88.7	66.9	60.7	102.3	218.0
1932					
January	93.8	70.2	64.4	103.5	233.4
February	102.0	83.2	79.3	105.4	212.9
March	113.8	96.7	94.9	107.6	214.9
April	96.1	88.1	84.7	107.5	143.3
May	91.0	89.2	86.1	106.9	98.7
June	91.2	90.8	88.0	106.8	93.6
July	83.5	82.4	78.2	106.0	90.4
August	90.9	91.5	88.8	106.9	87.6
September	92.2	93.3	90.8	107.5	85.3
October	96.1	100.2	98.7	108.5	71.8
November	111.8	115.9	116.9	110.3	87.3
December	131.3	134.9	138.9	111.9	109.8
1933					
January	135.1	141.0	146.2	111.6	100.3
February	145.3	152.7	160.6	107.4	101.5
March	167.9	179.7	192.4	107.6	98.1
April	154.9	168.6	179.7	105.5	73.7
May	153.1	169.2	180.4	105.0	58.0
June	148.4	164.6	175.3	103.4	52.4
July	135.6	150.6	159.0	102.3	47.3
August	140.4	156.1	165.5	102.4	47.4
September	134.3	149.5	157.8	101.8	44.4
October	145.6	163.3	174.1	101.6	40.5
November	153.9	173.3	185.7	102.7	39.2
December	123.5	136.9	142.6	104.3	44.2

[1] For absolute amounts see original source of data.
[2] Base values are as follows: Total public and private, $25,829,314; total public, $22,096,018; general public, $18,805,842; public special allowances, $3,290,176; and total private, $3,733,296.

Table 5.—Monthly Expenditures for Relief From Public and Private Funds in 120 Urban Areas, Expressed as Relative Numbers, January 1929–December 1935—Cont'd

[Average month 1931–1933=100]

| Year and month | Total public and private | Public | | | Total private |
		Total	General	Special allowances	
1934					
January	118.3	131.4	136.1	104.6	40.8
February	123.7	138.6	144.8	103.5	35.3
March	146.7	165.1	175.5	105.5	38.0
April	217.0	247.7	272.8	104.4	35.3
May	233.7	267.3	295.5	105.5	35.3
June	221.5	253.7	279.3	107.7	30.8
July	229.9	263.8	290.9	108.8	29.4
August	246.4	283.1	313.3	110.6	28.8
September	231.0	265.2	292.2	111.1	28.3
October	253.3	291.3	322.2	114.2	28.9
November	272.1	313.1	347.6	116.4	29.2
December	289.2	332.4	367.4	132.5	33.1
1935					
January	332.8	383.7	426.9	136.7	31.4
February	304.8	351.4	388.7	138.4	29.0
March	311.1	358.8	396.9	141.5	28.8
April	308.1	355.4	392.4	144.1	27.8
May	304.4	351.3	387.2	146.1	26.5
June	284.0	328.0	359.3	149.0	23.4
July	298.0	344.4	378.1	151.8	23.1
August	277.2	320.1	349.2	153.4	23.2
September	236.7	272.9	293.8	153.7	22.2
October	238.5	274.8	295.5	156.2	23.7
November	198.5	228.1	240.2	159.0	23.7
December	161.5	183.8	187.6	162.3	29.3

Source: Derived from absolute amounts published by Winslow, Emma A., *Trends in Different Types of Public and Private Relief in Urban Areas, 1929–35,* Publication No. 237, U. S. Department of Labor, Children's Bureau, 1937.

Table 6.—Indices of Monthly Expenditures for Outdoor Relief in Rural-Town Areas,[1] Urban Areas,[2] and Total United States, January 1932–December 1935

[Average month 1935=100]

Year	Rural-town areas [1]	Urban areas [2]	Total United States	Year	Rural-town areas [1]	Urban areas [2]	Total United States
1932				*1934*			
January	18.3	34.5	30.6	January	50.6	43.6	45.3
February	19.3	37.6	33.1	February	47.1	45.6	45.9
March	20.6	42.0	36.7	March	56.3	54.0	54.6
April	20.7	35.4	31.8	April	73.7	80.0	78.4
May	18.0	33.4	29.6	May	82.2	86.2	85.2
June	17.6	33.6	29.7	June	85.7	81.6	82.6
July	17.8	30.8	27.6	July	92.4	84.8	86.6
August	17.1	33.5	29.5	August	103.3	90.8	93.8
September	19.3	34.0	30.3	September	100.6	85.2	88.9
October	23.4	35.4	32.4	October	105.2	93.4	96.3
November	31.5	41.2	38.8	November	118.0	100.3	104.7
December	35.6	48.4	45.3	December	125.5	106.6	111.2
1933				*1935*			
January	42.8	49.6	47.9	January	139.2	122.7	126.7
February	43.6	53.4	50.9	February	130.6	112.4	116.9
March	47.4	61.7	58.1	March	128.0	114.8	118.0
April	47.9	56.9	54.7	April	122.9	113.6	115.9
May	46.6	56.2	53.9	May	119.1	112.2	113.9
June	42.1	54.5	51.4	June	101.2	104.7	103.8
July	51.1	49.8	50.1	July	96.3	109.9	106.5
August	54.4	51.6	52.3	August	89.0	102.2	98.9
September	50.0	49.3	49.5	September	73.3	87.2	83.8
October	58.3	53.5	54.7	October	76.9	87.9	85.2
November	63.7	56.6	58.3	November	68.1	73.1	71.9
December	50.3	45.3	46.5	December	55.1	59.5	58.3

[1] Represents counties containing no city of 25,000 or over, and Massachusetts and Connecticut townships of less than 5,000.
[2] Represents counties containing cities of 25,000 or over, and Massachusetts and Connecticut townships of 5,000 and over.

Source: Unpublished data from the Division of Social Research, Rural Section, Works Progress Administration. Indíces based on data from Rural-Town Relief Series and Urban Relief Series.

Table 7.—Summary of Expenditures for Public Outdoor Relief in Selected Areas, 1910–1935

Amount in thousands

Year	Financial Statistics of Cities U.S. Census 16 Cities	Mounting Bill for Relief Hurlin 36 Cities[1]	Cost of Relief in 16 Cities Clapp-USCB 16 Cities	Trends in Philanthropy in New Haven W. King	Financial Trends in Organized Social Work in New York City K. Huntley	New York State Department of Social Welfare	Indiana State Board of Charities	Special Report U.S. Census 308 Cities	U.S. Children's Bureau 120 Urban Areas	WPA Division of Social Research 385 Rural-Town Areas	WPA Division of Social Research Rural-Urban U.S. (estimated)
1910	—	—	—	$16	$229	$885	$266	—	—	—	—
1911	$1,559	—	—	17	241	921	271	—	—	—	—
1912	1,700	—	—	18	248	945	306	—	—	—	—
1913	(3)	—	—	16	253	956	302	—	—	—	—
1914	(3)	—	—	15	223	1,084	303	—	—	—	—
1915	(3)	—	—	14	256	1,277	435	—	—	—	—
1916	(3)	$1,685	—	16	646	1,158	391	—	—	—	—
1917	3,488	1,904	—	15	1,472	2,107	427	—	—	—	—
1918	3,980	2,071	—	17	2,087	3,094	426	—	—	—	—
1919	6,183	2,386	—	28	2,391	3,653	388	—	—	—	—
1920	(3)	2,957	—	51	2,981	4,351	417	—	—	—	—
1921	(3)	5,343	—	79	4,140	5,703	610	—	—	—	—
1922	(3)	4,742	—	92	4,932	7,252	741	—	—	—	—
1923	11,640	3,877	—	97	4,984	7,278	524	—	—	—	—
1924	12,818	4,553	$4,671	111	5,316	7,799	619	—	—	—	—
1925	14,709	5,301	—	112	5,662	8,548	841	—	—	—	—
1926	14,814	—	—	—	5,909	8,966	(3)	—	—	—	—
1927	17,059	—	—	—	6,301	10,036	1,104	—	—	—	—
1928	20,014	—	—	—	7,293	11,789	(3)	—	—	—	—
1929	18,989	—	7,636	—	7,750	13,083	1,446	[2]$10,802	$33,449	—	—
1930	28,004	—	—	—	9,271	17,786	2,506	[2]34,201	—	—	—
1931	64,142	—	—	—	31,665	41,277	4,681	—	123,320	—	—
1932	(3)	—	—	—	57,870	88,203	(3)	—	251,104	$10,223	$446,846
1933	(3)	—	—	—	[4]101,211	[4]156,376	(3)	—	[4]421,032	[4]22,688	[4]802,423
1934	(3)	—	—	—	[4]169,316	[4]215,601	(3)	—	[4]652,467	[4]39,664	[4]1,287,139
1935	(3)	—	—	—	(3)	(3)	(3)	—	[5]829,224	[5]45,608	[5]1,595,694

[1] Figures interpolated; selected agencies in these cities.
[2] Figures are for the first quarter of year.
[3] Figures not available or not available in comparable form.
[4] Excludes CWA expenditures.
[5] Excludes Works Program expenditures.

Source: Compiled from sources indicated in table heading. Full source references given in Part I, p. 5 ff.

Table 8.—Obligations Incurred per Inhabitant [1] for Relief Extended to Cases, General Relief Program, FERA, by States,[2] Quarterly Intervals, July 1933–October 1935

State and geographic division	July 1933	October 1933	January 1934	April 1934	July 1934	October 1934	January 1935	April 1935	July 1935	October 1935
United States total	$0.45	$0.48	$0.36	$0.70	$0.77	$0.90	$1.16	$1.04	$0.93	$0.74
New England:										
Maine	.40	.36	.33	.84	.64	.78	.87	.80	.67	.57
New Hampshire	.20	.26	.32	.53	.37	.56	.55	.93	.79	.63
Vermont	.23	.16	.11	.31	.32	.37	.62	.65	.48	.18
Massachusetts	.70	.63	.52	1.11	1.21	1.42	1.85	1.77	1.69	1.48
Rhode Island	.49	.41	.21	.76	.69	.78	1.11	.89	.80	.85
Connecticut	.42	.38	.26	.79	.66	.83	1.11	1.07	.99	.82
Middle Atlantic:										
New York	.85	.91	.57	1.61	1.61	1.72	1.95	1.86	1.85	1.19
New Jersey	.46	.47	.48	1.21	.89	1.21	1.23	1.12	1.03	.94
Pennsylvania	.70	.67	.67	1.09	.89	1.02	1.75	1.73	1.54	1.41
East North Central:										
Ohio	.53	.50	.28	.68	.81	.95	1.35	1.11	1.24	.72
Indiana	.31	.36	.21	.44	.59	.86	1.01	.92	.62	.30
Illinois	.66	.75	.54	.77	1.02	1.07	1.44	1.26	1.06	1.01
Michigan	.57	.75	.46	.68	.82	1.22	1.38	1.02	.94	.90
Wisconsin	.51	.48	.37	.71	1.04	1.23	1.37	1.18	.99	.81
West North Central:										
Minnesota	.24	.28	.27	.66	.84	1.11	1.49	1.25	.92	.76
Iowa	.20	.22	.11	.23	.39	.43	.63	.53	.34	.33
Missouri	.22	.21	.17	.33	.40	.59	.81	.69	.58	.52
North Dakota	.16	.33	.71	1.72	.95	1.63	1.84	1.84	.94	.84
South Dakota	.21	.67	.88	1.00	1.93	2.43	2.34	1.94	.71	.55
Nebraska	.07	.15	.18	.42	.35	.65	.96	.89	.59	.58
Kansas	.27	.27	.10	.36	.51	.72	1.17	1.01	.69	.68
South Atlantic:										
Delaware	.74	.59	.69	.33	.35	.38	.42	.31	.36	.26
Maryland	.41	.56	.61	.94	.72	.75	.90	.79	.61	.56
District of Columbia	.42	.59	.28	1.19	.94	1.16	1.17	1.04	.93	.66
Virginia	.04	.05	.06	.06	.15	.17	.24	.32	.32	.23
West Virginia	.62	.68	.40	.34	.64	.75	.96	.76	.62	.62
North Carolina	.16	.15	.15	.18	.22	.21	.32	.28	.25	.20
South Carolina	.31	.51	.13	.38	.37	.53	.37	.23	.23	.10
Georgia	.10	.32	.18	.28	.31	.39	.38	.41	.30	.21
Florida	.35	.80	.11	1.06	.84	.88	.68	.45	.34	.30
East South Central:										
Kentucky	.27	.20	.32	.15	.26	.33	.42	.42	.36	.33
Tennessee	.12	.13	.09	.14	.44	.19	.36	.43	.27	.17
Alabama	.16	.37	.25	.33	.42	.38	.37	.37	.41	.25
Mississippi	.14	.18	.34	.30	.42	.32	.47	.32	.29	.30
West South Central:										
Arkansas	.18	.27	.38	.07	.29	.49	.50	.39	.45	.15
Louisiana	.44	.52	.74	.50	.51	.51	.58	.64	.65	.41
Oklahoma	.22	.30	.10	.33	.29	.52	.63	.37	.33	.36
Texas	.22	.16	.12	.24	.39	.49	.74	.52	.33	.23
Mountain:										
Montana	.53	.50	.47	1.22	1.22	1.38	1.86	1.35	1.03	.68
Idaho	.27	.13	.20	.44	.40	.80	1.35	1.03	.74	.57
Wyoming	.09	.09	.07	.49	.76	1.03	.92	.89	.74	.33
Colorado	.35	.29	.15	.77	1.26	1.40	1.72	1.42	1.13	.88
New Mexico	.06	.08	.23	.38	1.41	.93	1.69	.90	.82	.54
Arizona	.62	.62	.46	.91	1.09	1.13	1.14	1.29	1.16	.81
Utah	.42	.46	.43	.79	1.03	1.47	1.63	1.50	1.06	.91
Nevada	.32	.33	.19	.30	.90	1.45	1.91	1.38	1.07	.47
Pacific:										
Washington	.60	.39	.37	.57	.61	.51	.88	.79	.76	.57
Oregon	.32	.22	.30	.50	.68	.72	1.09	.80	.62	.37
California	.53	.40	.24	.51	.82	.92	1.67	1.59	1.55	1.44

[1] Based on population estimates of the Bureau of the Census.
[2] Includes the District of Columbia.

Source: Compiled from official data on obligations incurred as reported to the Division of Research, Statistics, and Finance of the Federal Emergency Relief Administration.
Note: This table was based on latest revised figures available at the date of analysis, November 1936.

Table 9.—Percent of Population [1] Receiving Relief, General Relief Program, FERA, by States,[2] Quarterly Intervals, July 1933–October 1935

State and geographic division	July 1933	October 1933	January 1934	April 1934	July 1934	October 1934	January 1935	April 1935	July 1935	October 1935
United States total	12.2	10.8	8.7	13.2	13.5	14.2	15.8	14.8	12.7	10.5
New England:										
Maine	6.5	5.7	4.8	10.9	7.5	8.8	10.1	10.8	12.1	9.2
New Hampshire	7.8	6.5	6.0	8.4	5.3	6.6	7.4	11.2	9.6	7.9
Vermont	4.9	3.1	3.2	6.3	5.4	5.6	8.7	9.0	8.6	4.3
Massachusetts	9.1	8.5	7.2	13.0	13.6	14.7	16.4	16.7	16.3	14.2
Rhode Island	8.9	7.3	4.5	10.1	10.3	11.1	11.4	11.6	10.9	10.1
Connecticut	8.5	6.7	5.8	12.5	8.9	10.3	11.5	11.1	10.0	8.6
Middle Atlantic:										
New York	11.6	10.4	7.6	16.2	15.4	15.3	16.8	16.3	15.0	10.5
New Jersey	10.2	8.9	8.1	16.4	12.5	13.8	15.0	14.3	12.7	11.2
Pennsylvania	18.8	15.4	14.6	15.7	15.3	15.4	17.9	18.5	17.4	16.4
East North Central:										
Ohio	14.2	12.0	8.8	14.8	14.1	16.2	18.1	16.7	15.8	12.6
Indiana	9.3	10.1	6.3	11.4	10.7	12.5	14.4	13.5	11.5	7.3
Illinois	12.8	11.0	8.8	13.0	13.7	13.6	14.7	14.3	12.2	12.1
Michigan	12.5	13.9	11.8	13.2	12.3	16.0	17.1	14.1	12.8	11.8
Wisconsin	10.7	9.1	6.9	12.1	12.7	13.8	15.9	14.3	11.4	10.8
West North Central:										
Minnesota	6.4	5.8	5.2	16.3	16.4	16.8	18.5	16.3	11.4	9.6
Iowa	6.9	5.8	3.3	7.1	8.9	8.6	10.8	9.8	6.5	5.6
Missouri	6.6	5.6	5.0	9.8	11.7	14.7	16.5	15.2	11.5	11.8
North Dakota	5.5	9.2	19.6	32.0	21.2	28.3	29.7	30.5	20.0	16.1
South Dakota	6.1	16.2	16.7	30.8	35.4	35.9	40.1	36.7	12.0	9.0
Nebraska	4.3	5.4	4.9	8.6	7.7	11.6	15.3	13.1	9.2	7.8
Kansas	11.2	9.4	3.8	10.9	11.4	14.6	17.4	17.5	12.1	11.8
South Atlantic:										
Delaware	14.2	9.1	10.2	11.8	6.4	6.6	7.2	6.2	6.0	4.2
Maryland	8.2	8.0	10.3	15.0	10.4	9.8	11.4	10.9	7.9	7.6
District of Columbia	7.5	9.4	5.1	12.6	11.4	11.9	12.0	10.6	8.5	5.6
Virginia	2.8	2.6	3.3	4.9	6.3	6.8	8.2	9.0	8.2	6.1
West Virginia	30.5	23.6	14.0	14.4	18.9	20.3	22.4	20.9	20.0	17.4
North Carolina	9.8	7.8	9.6	9.5	9.8	7.8	10.0	9.7	8.0	6.3
South Carolina	21.0	22.8	8.7	15.8	15.4	18.0	14.7	10.7	8.1	5.0
Georgia	6.6	9.7	6.2	8.7	10.0	12.0	10.4	9.7	7.3	4.2
Florida	23.7	26.8	6.2	21.4	23.3	22.6	18.5	12.9	12.5	10.4
East South Central:										
Kentucky	20.0	13.1	13.8	11.5	16.3	15.8	17.5	18.0	16.6	15.3
Tennessee	9.5	7.2	4.3	10.1	13.1	10.0	11.2	12.0	10.5	8.1
Alabama	14.6	17.5	13.1	16.9	14.3	12.1	8.5	8.6	9.4	6.7
Mississippi	14.0	10.0	14.7	12.8	14.9	11.8	13.7	9.4	7.9	7.3
West South Central:										
Arkansas	11.2	12.1	16.2	5.8	10.2	13.0	17.8	12.2	11.4	4.6
Louisiana	13.5	14.9	18.6	10.3	9.2	9.0	8.4	9.0	9.6	8.7
Oklahoma	20.1	19.0	8.0	17.0	18.5	23.2	26.5	22.6	17.1	15.3
Texas	13.6	7.8	7.0	13.0	15.0	16.0	18.9	15.3	9.7	7.0
Mountain:										
Montana	15.2	12.5	11.0	17.9	17.9	17.5	20.3	20.1	15.5	10.4
Idaho	8.5	4.2	5.7	12.2	10.7	13.6	22.0	20.0	12.7	10.0
Wyoming	2.7	2.5	2.3	9.1	12.8	11.2	15.4	16.0	7.9	5.1
Colorado	13.2	10.7	9.5	18.7	19.5	19.8	22.8	21.2	15.7	12.6
New Mexico	6.1	6.0	9.8	14.2	28.1	25.3	33.7	26.7	28.9	21.2
Arizona	23.1	18.6	12.1	23.5	26.9	23.6	23.5	22.6	20.9	15.3
Utah	19.8	13.8	11.9	20.7	21.0	21.2	24.0	24.2	18.6	16.5
Nevada	6.1	5.5	3.5	-5.4	7.5	9.9	13.1	10.2	7.4	4.9
Pacific:										
Washington	14.4	8.5	7.9	12.2	11.0	10.3	13.1	12.9	12.4	8.5
Oregon	8.0	5.7	7.3	10.0	10.4	9.6	13.6	12.3	8.2	5.5
California	9.9	8.8	5.4	9.3	10.3	11.1	14.4	13.8	12.2	10.4

[1] Based on estimates of the Bureau of the Census.
[2] Includes the District of Columbia.

Source: Compiled from official data on case loads as reported to the Division of Research, Statistics, and Finance of the Federal Emergency Relief Administration.
Note: This table was based on latest revised figures available at the date of analysis, November 1936.

Table 10.—Average Monthly Relief Benefit per Family Case,[1] General Relief Program, FERA, by States,[2] Quarterly Intervals, July 1933–October 1935

State and geographic division	July 1933	October 1933	January 1934	April 1934	July 1934	October 1934	January 1935	April 1935	July 1935	October 1935
United States total	$15.51	$19.08	$17.15	$22.12	$24.34	$26.43	$30.45	$28.96	$29.64	$27.84
New England:										
Maine	26.21	27.36	29.09	35.94	36.82	39.97	38.26	31.44	24.52	26.47
New Hampshire	10.06	15.73	19.64	26.20	25.94	35.04	28.58	33.88	31.52	32.70
Vermont	20.94	21.52	15.36	22.49	27.74	29.44	32.20	32.24	24.60	20.53
Massachusetts	32.27	31.22	29.35	34.32	37.22	40.07	47.84	44.97	44.50	46.02
Rhode Island	23.54	26.79	19.60	31.21	30.68	30.78	43.05	34.04	32.13	36.52
Connecticut	21.30	24.70	18.61	27.49	33.27	35.54	43.38	44.43	45.44	43.48
Middle Atlantic:										
New York	30.59	37.16	32.16	41.64	44.93	46.92	47.91	46.31	49.06	43.39
New Jersey	19.86	23.78	25.12	30.06	29.98	35.77	33.30	31.55	31.96	32.82
Pennsylvania	17.81	20.87	21.55	32.79	27.35	29.53	42.50	40.18	37.80	36.52
East North Central:										
Ohio	15.70	17.91	13.03	19.23	24.19	24.24	30.60	26.71	31.15	22.05
Indiana	12.58	15.47	12.54	16.15	22.87	28.59	28.65	27.82	21.73	15.22
Illinois	20.77	26.84	22.45	22.34	28.14	28.41	35.06	30.99	29.42	27.26
Michigan	19.80	23.72	15.90	21.50	28.17	31.88	32.73	29.49	29.58	30.54
Wisconsin	21.87	23.77	24.23	20.43	36.06	38.16	36.94	35.63	36.53	30.72
West North Central:										
Minnesota	16.46	20.81	20.78	17.33	22.78	29.26	34.82	31.86	32.03	30.82
Iowa	12.91	16.85	12.73	13.38	18.37	21.01	25.36	22.99	22.18	25.28
Missouri	14.88	14.57	12.22	13.33	14.06	16.12	20.20	18.53	18.61	17.24
North Dakota	13.32	16.26	17.15	25.51	21.09	27.63	29.08	28.81	22.11	25.22
South Dakota	14.17	18.07	19.07	13.73	23.17	27.93	25.04	22.53	23.34	24.27
Nebraska	6.55	12.56	14.87	20.92	19.03	23.49	26.59	26.83	25.18	28.03
Kansas	9.25	11.31	8.94	13.67	18.45	19.72	26.95	23.40	22.10	21.88
South Atlantic:										
Delaware	22.76	26.21	26.04	13.11	21.06	22.82	23.20	19.40	25.14	22.78
Maryland	22.26	30.91	25.56	26.61	29.46	32.69	33.54	30.14	31.95	30.95
District of Columbia	20.00	21.57	20.64	35.71	30.09	32.73	37.61	32.00	41.24	44.81
Virginia	6.94	8.60	7.93	5.69	11.13	12.10	13.91	16.88	17.65	16.64
West Virginia	9.22	12.95	12.01	10.71	14.94	16.40	18.82	15.82	13.37	15.07
North Carolina	7.64	8.75	6.95	8.65	10.60	12.01	14.93	13.80	14.32	14.44
South Carolina	5.61	10.18	6.13	10.52	10.43	12.96	11.08	9.41	12.27	8.41
Georgia	5.88	13.49	11.95	13.19	13.19	13.72	15.02	16.90	16.63	20.07
Florida	5.58	11.92	6.64	19.14	13.82	14.41	13.99	13.18	10.06	10.26
East South Central:										
Kentucky	6.40	7.18	10.33	6.09	7.51	9.79	11.26	11.00	10.13	9.93
Tennessee	5.87	8.45	8.66	6.35	15.61	8.98	14.49	16.75	11.60	9.46
Alabama	5.19	10.06	7.94	8.78	12.81	13.22	18.06	17.34	17.70	16.13
Mississippi	3.83	7.65	9.28	9.44	11.12	10.14	13.56	13.10	12.96	14.30
West South Central:										
Arkansas	6.44	8.97	9.28	5.00	12.33	16.28	12.57	13.42	16.35	13.05
Louisiana	13.89	15.41	18.46	21.64	22.54	24.25	26.71	27.68	26.17	18.30
Oklahoma	4.38	6.14	4.95	8.41	7.35	10.32	11.16	7.50	8.79	10.38
Texas	6.93	8.59	6.76	7.83	11.07	13.18	16.97	14.61	13.92	11.19
Mountain:										
Montana	13.31	15.38	15.20	25.30	25.72	32.26	36.62	26.89	27.38	26.77
Idaho	11.91	11.70	12.65	13.84	15.50	24.94	25.03	20.84	23.91	22.56
Wyoming	11.93	12.11	11.46	22.80	23.15	37.80	24.53	22.35	34.24	26.08
Colorado	10.56	10.61	5.70	17.08	26.83	29.02	30.69	26.52	28.38	27.84
New Mexico	4.37	5.57	10.05	12.55	22.10	16.31	22.12	14.77	12.40	10.73
Arizona	10.20	13.88	14.55	15.65	16.26	19.36	19.58	23.55	24.99	23.97
Utah	9.85	15.39	14.87	17.28	21.45	30.33	29.84	26.93	24.58	23.73
Nevada	13.64	18.27	14.22	17.30	33.24	39.61	48.84	44.00	46.27	30.43
Pacific:										
Washington	15.96	17.90	16.96	18.18	21.10	19.54	25.18	23.43	23.21	25.58
Oregon	14.19	14.34	13.66	17.84	24.31	26.64	30.33	24.38	26.80	24.77
California	18.77	19.62	17.93	19.97	29.95	32.09	40.00	41.39	45.38	48.34

[1] Based on a net unduplicated count of relief cases; some cases received both direct and work relief during a given month, either successively or concurrently.
[2] Includes the District of Columbia.

Source: Compiled from official data on obligations incurred and case loads as reported to the Division of Research, Statistics, and Finance of the Federal Emergency Relief Administration.
Note: This table was based on latest revised figures available at the date of analysis, November 1936.

Appendix B

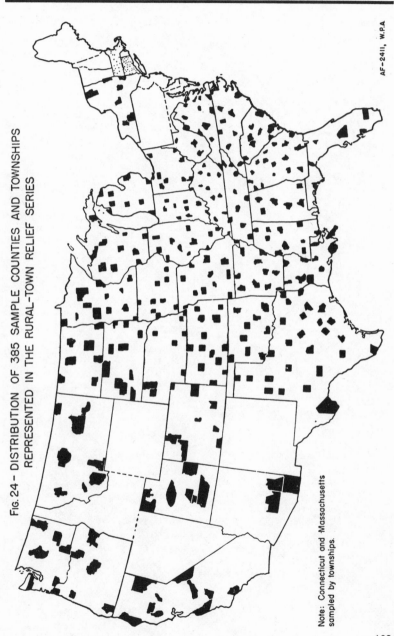

Fig. 24– DISTRIBUTION OF 385 SAMPLE COUNTIES AND TOWNSHIPS REPRESENTED IN THE RURAL–TOWN RELIEF SERIES

AF–2411, W.P.A

Note: Connecticut and Massachusetts sampled by townships.

Appendix C

FEDERAL GOVERNMENT UNITS PARTICI-
PATING IN THE WORKS PROGRAM,
DECEMBER 31, 1935[1]

Legislative Establishments:
    Library of Congress
Executive Departments:
    Department of Agriculture
        Bureau of Agricultural Engineering
        Bureau of Animal Industry
        Bureau of Biological Survey
        Bureau of Entomology and Plant Quarantine
        Bureau of Chemistry and Soils
        Bureau of Dairy Industry
        Bureau of Plant Industry
        Bureau of Public Roads
        Extension Service
        Forest Service
        Soil Conservation Service
        Weather Bureau
    Department of Commerce
        Bureau of the Census
        Bureau of Fisheries
        Bureau of Lighthouses
        National Bureau of Standards

---

[1] This list was compiled from the following sources: *The Report of the President of the United States to the Congress of the Operations under the Emergency Relief Appropriation Act of 1935, January 9, 1936; Report on the Works Program, March 16, 1936;* and *United States Government Manual, 1936.*

Executive Departments—Continued.
    Department of the Interior
        Alaska Road Commission
        All-American Canal
        Bureau of Reclamation
        Bituminous Coal Commission
        Geological Survey
        National Park Service
        Office of Education
        Puerto Rico Reconstruction Administration
        St. Elizabeths Hospital
        Temporary Government of the Virgin Islands
    Department of Justice
    Department of Labor
        Bureau of Immigration and Naturalization
        Bureau of Labor Statistics
        United States Employment Service
    Department of the Navy
        Bureau of Yards and Docks
    Department of the Treasury
        Bureau of Internal Revenue
        Bureau of Public Health Service
        Coast Guard
        Procurement Division
    Department of War
        Office of the Chief of Engineers
        Office of the Quartermaster General
Independent Establishments:
    Advisory Committee on Allotments
    Alley Dwelling Authority
    Civil Service Commission
    Emergency Conservation Work
    Employees' Compensation Commission
    Federal Emergency Administration of Public Works (PWA)
        Non-Federal Division
        Housing Division
    Federal Emergency Relief Administration
    General Accounting Office
    National Emergency Council
    National Resources Committee
    Prison Industries Reorganization Administration
    Resettlement Administration
    Rural Electrification Administration
    Veterans' Administration
    Works Progress Administration

Appendix D

METHODOLOGICAL NOTE ON THE ESTIMATES OF EXPENDITURES FOR CATEGORICAL RELIEF IN THE UNITED STATES, 1933–1935

ESTIMATES OF the amounts expended in the United States during 1933, 1934, and 1935 for aid to the aged, aid to the blind, and aid to dependent children are based on State data available from various sources. State expenditures for old-age relief in 1933 and 1934 and partial data for 1935 were obtained from surveys made by the United States Bureau of Labor Statistics. Data on State expenditures for blind relief for 1933 were obtained largely from the American Foundation for the Blind, and for 1934 and 1935 from annual surveys made by the United States Bureau of Labor Statistics. Comprehensive data on aid to dependent children were available only for the years 1931 and 1934 from surveys made by the United States Children's Bureau. Information from the above sources was supplemented by data collected or published by State Departments of Welfare or in State Treasurers' reports. In some instances it was necessary to adjust data from a fiscal to a calendar year basis and to include some estimated figures to build up annual State totals for each category of relief.

For those years for which expenditure data were not available—i. e., aid to dependent children in 1933 and 1935—annual totals were estimated by using existing annual figures and applying the percentage change indicated by the Children's Bureau Urban Relief Series for that category of relief.[1]

---

[1] See Part I, p. 29, for a description of this series, and table 14 for relative numbers indicating trends in categorical relief since January 1929.

After the annual totals for the United States were obtained by combining the State data for each category, monthly estimates were derived by spreading the expenditures over the months in accordance with trends established for the 120 areas included in the Urban Relief Series. Because of differences in data available for the three types of relief, the procedure followed in adjusting monthly expenditures varied somewhat,[2] but in every case the urban relief trends were used to check the accuracy of the estimates. Use of this trend as an adjustment factor was believed to be justified by the fact that a very substantial share of the total volume of relief to special classes during these years was extended in the 120 urban areas represented in the series. The adjusted figures are undoubtedly more accurate than could be secured by spreading annual expenditures evenly over the months.

The resulting estimates are necessarily rough, but they are believed to give a fairly adequate measure of the trend and volume of categorical assistance in the United States as a whole during the 3-year period. It is apparent from the trends shown in Part I that expenditures for aid to the aged, to the blind, and to dependent children are remarkably stable except as they are affected by new State legislation. A list of recent laws providing for old-age relief and aid to dependent children in an additional number of States is given in Part I. The effect of these laws is reflected in the monthly estimates.

Estimates of expenditures in individual States are not presented here since they are necessarily imperfect, and in some cases they undoubtedly represent serious understatement or overstatement of expenditures. It is believed, however, that these errors tend to cancel each other in the estimates for total United States.

Source materials used in constructing the estimates are listed below:

Aid to the Aged:

1. Parker, Florence E., "Experience Under State Old-Age Pension Act of 1934," *Monthly Labor Review*, August 1935. Also reprint of same article, U. S. Bureau of Labor Statistics, Serial No. R 270.

2. Unpublished data supplied by Bureau of Labor Statistics, Summary of Operations Under Old-Age Pension Acts, 1935.

3. Economic Security Act, *Hearings before the Committee on Ways and Means, H. R., 1935*, Table 14, "Operation of Old-Age Pension Laws of the United States, 1934," p. 77.

Aid to the Blind:

1. Unpublished data supplied by the American Foundation for the Blind, Inc., New York City.

---

[2] For example, monthly estimates for old-age relief expenditures during 1933 and 1934 were adjusted according to case-load data for old-age relief during those years.

2. *Public Provision for Pensions for the Blind in 1934*, Serial No. R 257, U. S. Bureau of Labor Statistics.

3. *Public Pensions for the Blind*, Serial No. R 422, U. S. Bureau of Labor Statistics.

4. State of Illinois, *Biennial Report of the Treasurer*, 1934.

5. State of Wisconsin, *Blind Pensions in Wisconsin, 1907–1934*.

Aid to Dependent Children:

1. *Mothers' Aid, 1931*, Publication No. 220, U. S. Children's Bureau.

2. Economic Security Act, *Hearings before the Committee on Ways and Means, H. R., 1935*, Table 18, "Estimated Number of Families and Children Receiving Mothers' Aid and Estimated Expenditures for this Purpose," p. 80. (Based on figures of November 1934 from U. S. Children's Bureau.)

Index

INDEX

113